VOICES FROM THE NORTH CAROLINA MOUNTAINS

VOICES FROM THE NORTH CAROLINA MOUNTAINS

APPALACHIAN ORAL HISTORIES

LYNN SALSI

THE
History
PRESS

Published by The History Press
Charleston, SC 29403
www.historypress.net

Cover image: Photo by Dana Blanton of Full Sun Farm in Big Sandy Mush, North Carolina.

First published 2007

Manufactured in the United States

ISBN 978.1.59629.230.7

Library of Congress Cataloging-in-Publication Data

Voices from the North Carolina mountains : Appalachian oral histories / [interviewed by] Lynn Salsi.
    p. cm.
  ISBN-13: 978-1-59629-230-7 (alk. paper)
1. Mountain life--North Carolina. 2. Mountain life--Appalachian Region, Southern.
3. Appalachians (People)--North Carolina--Interviews. 4. North Carolina--Social life and customs. 5. Appalachian Region, Southern--Social life and customs.
6. North Carolina--Biography. 7. Appalachian Region, Southern--Biography. 8. Interviews--North Carolina. 9. Interviews--Appalachian Region, Southern. 10. Oral history. I. Salsi, Lynn, 1947-
  F262.A16V65 2007
  975.6'8040922--dc22
                                2007016097

Notice: The information in this book is true and complete to the best of our knowledge. It is offered without guarantee on the part of the author or The History Press. The author and The History Press disclaim all liability in connection with the use of this book.

For Burke

The Blue Ridge Parkway is a stone's throw from Blowing Rock, Boone, Creston, Sugar Grove and communities where mountain traditions flourish. Constructed in the 1930s, travelers come to view scenic wonders and enjoy Southern hospitality. *Photo by Salsi.*

CONTENTS

The Linn Cove Viaduct was constructed to hang from the slopes of Grandfather Mountain. As an engineering wonder, its S-shape used every geometric alignment known in bridge building when it was completed in 1983. *Photo by B. Salsi.*

ACKNOWLEDGEMENTS

The first thank-you goes to Burke Salsi for his photographs of people, places and things. Thanks to Bo and Brian Salsi, Jay, Maria and Morgan Elizabeth Swygert.

Special thanks to those who participated in the telling of these wonderful stories. Amy Michels was generous in meeting with me many times. I received lessons about food gathering, visiting neighbors and listening to old mountain music in the living room of her home. Thanks to her husband, Alfred, master instrument builder. He and Amy farm their land using old ways. Glenn Bolick, keeper of mountain tradition and lore, has been helpful on all my Blue Ridge Mountain projects since 1998. He imparted information about music, buck dancing, plowing days and mowing days. Eula Osborne had clear memories of her grandmother, of farming and sidelights about her ancestors. Ora Watson is well known and loved by thousands of people. I met her when she was only ninety-one at the weekly senior citizens music jam in Boone and Cove Creek. We've talked a lot about her life and times. At the age of ninety-five, she's still playing the fiddle. Clyde Lewis and his wife Ruth have dedicated their lives to farming and both have had many chores since they were little.

Thanks to Steve Kruger of the Avery County Historical Society; Kim Cumber, archivist, North Carolina Office of Archives and History; Steve Massengill, retired archivist, North Carolina Office of Archives and History; the Appalachian Writer's Association and Dr. Lee Tobin McClain of Seton Hill University.

Thanks to David Weatherly and Roy Ackland of WGHP, the FOX affiliate in High Point, North Carolina, for their unfailing support in keeping the history and traditions of North Carolina alive through their interviews and special events that are intertwined with "Roy's Folks."

Many thanks to those who value oral history, including Connie Mason, maritime heritage tourism officer with the North Carolina Department of Commerce; Cindy Hamilton of the Carteret County Historical Society; Judy Morton of Action Greensboro and Vicki Jarrell, editor of *Our State* magazine.

Others who play a part in my North Carolina history projects include Cindy Kane of Guilford Technical Community College; Lewis Edwards of Randolph Community College; Mary Kay Forbes, retired fourth-grade teacher of Guilford and Rowan Counties; Jan Hensley, photographic historian; James Young, illustrator of *Young Ray Hicks Learns the Jack Tales*; Mary Young of Art Quest; Jean Cone and Jan Broadfoot of Broadfoot's of Wendell; Melody Watson, blogger and website designer; Lois Mendenhall of Parnassus Book Distributors and author Adrea Peters.

A special thank-you to Kirsty Sutton, Lee Handford and Katie Parry at The History Press.

Editor's Note: I am grateful for the cooperation of those who shared their stories and their enthusiasm for this project. I did not tamper with their voices, yet I placed events in chronological order and edited to clarify details. These oral histories were not transcriptions. They were recorded in longhand to accommodate the interviewees who are not professional public speakers. Without a tape player, they felt free to speak.

INTRODUCTION

This book chronicles life in the bygone days in the Blue Ridge Mountains of Western North Carolina. More importantly, it is told by members of the last generation who remember what life was like with no paved roads and no electricity. All are local talkers who honor their ancestors by keeping stories of the old days alive. They all enjoy talking about the weather, what they planted and special events such as molasses boilings, mowing days and weddings.

There are many western counties bordering Tennessee. The personal stories included in this volume represent Caldwell, Avery, Ashe and Watauga Counties. The Blue Ridge Mountains are rich in the history, culture and tradition of the first settlers who arrived to escape the Revolutionary War. Then others traveled into Indian Territory—the first western frontier—seeking farmland. These stories make legends and history real as they apply to the everyday lives of grandparents, parents and neighbors.

The voices and images within reflect the tradition of passing knowledge from one generation to another. The old way of doing things lingers with fewer and fewer people as new generations come forth into a technological age, and as the mountains swell with migrating retirees, vacationers and buyers of second homes. There is something unnatural about seeing original mountain people blending into a landscape of paved roads, housing developments, shopping centers and Wal-Mart.

Strong voices from the mountains arose from isolation. The people who settled there in the late 1700s knew they were entering Indian Territory. Some families preserved oral histories of that time. The first people, subsequent generations and others who settled in the 1800s supported themselves mostly through subsistence farming and raising livestock. Some, like Daniel Boone, engaged in the fur trade and sought areas where wild game abounded. According to the Bolick and Hicks families, few of their ancestors owned a gun and none participated in the fur business, because it was itinerate. "Farmers had to stay home to take care of plantin', hoein' and harvestin'. Hunters had to travel too far," Glenn Bolick said. Most professional hunters came through the Blue Ridge Mountains seasonally. By the mid 1800s, most had made their way to Kentucky and Tennessee.

Rural, traditional and superstitious ways were preserved until World War II. The Appalachian people weren't convenienced until they got electricity in 1946 and 1947. Even though towns like Boone and Blowing Rock were tourist destinations as early as 1850, the roads remained narrow and rough until the late 1940s. Tradition, suspicion, stubbornness, politics and lack of cash caused "new ways" to be slow in coming for regular folks.

The people included in this volume have stories to tell about the way it was for themselves, their families, their communities and their ancestors. They all treasure the practical old ways of doing things and continue working to carry on mountain traditions. They never took the easy way out. Their life in the mountains now helps to educate future generations.

It is with satisfaction I present farmers, sawyers, taletellers, musicians, balladeers, talkers and dancers who enrich their communities and the Appalachian Mountains by sharing their family traditions. The incredible beauty of the area, the fine highways, the Blue Ridge Parkway, the vistas and tourist attractions are only a backdrop for a special culture that must never be forgotten.

AMY MICHELS
BANJO PICKER, FOWL FARMER
AND COON HUNTER

I got to the North Carolina mountains when I was still a young'un. Our church had a youth magazine with a section about summer mission programs. There were descriptions about different places we could go. That was in the 1970s when there was talk about how people livin' in the Appalachian Mountains needed help. Yet, that was not the reason I wanted to go. Churches all over the United States sent summer youth mission groups to help people. I'd never seen the mountains except in photographs. I knew I wanted to go there.

I came on a Trailways bus. I was excited about the trip and was anxious to get to Valle Crucis. As we went along, some people got off and others got on. The closer we got to Banners Elk and Boone, the more relaxed I felt,'cause people were friendly and more like country folk. The talk started shiftin' to gardens and quilts and sech.

HELPIN' OTHERS

I picked the Valle Crucis Mission School. I packed my clothes and took my banjo and became part of a group that spent six weeks goin' around helpin' elderly people, meetin' mountain people, helpin' farmers and lookin' at crafts. There were also social activities held at the church school. We had barn dances with live string-band music. There was hikin' on mountain trails and swimmin' in the creek.

Alfred and Amy were married in Boone. The talented musicians love the mountains, simple living and playing music. Alfred makes fine string instruments including violins, fiddles, cellos and basses. *Photograph courtesy of the Michels collection.*

Everything was mostly centered on helpin' people. All the young'uns in the program worked in the farm fields, and met families—particularly old people—that followed old-timey traditions. The fieldwork was hard, but I liked being outside. I had a little experience detasselin' corn the summer before, so I knew a lot about being a farmhand.

I enjoyed everything, especially the people that liked sittin' around in the evenin' to tell tales and play ole music on all kinds of instruments, includin' homemade ones. They always seemed so glad for company. I was tickled to take my banjo and sit around and learn new tunes. I always enjoyed bein' with older people.

Banjo Player

My mother got me a guitar with Green Stamps when I was about ten years old because I wanted to learn to play an instrument. I taught myself chords and went to the public library and checked out records to hear different kinds of music. My friend had a banjo. When I heard it, I decided I liked that sound better.

When Amy arrived in Valle Crucis, North Carolina, in the 1970s, she learned about farm life and liked it so much, she stayed. Alfred Michels is pictured with his horse-drawn lime speader. *Photograph courtesy of the Michels collection.*

My friend played bluegrass, but I thought it sounded too modern. I learned to play "Shortnin' Bread" and "Bile Them Cabbage Down." That's about the time I got a banjo and noticed how people played with different styles. I played without a pick by kinda usin' my thumb to knock out tunes. But when I asked around to get better doin' it, everybody said I had to have a pick. There was no way to play a banjo without a pick.

We lived near a barn that had dances and sometimes some of us would go over and listen to the music. One night I was there and the banjo player was not usin' picks. When he took a break, I got the banjo player aside and asked him to show me how to do a few licks. He didn't mind. It didn't take me long to play claw-hammer style without a pick. It was a simple technique; I just had to practice.

Years later, I still like to play music. It's a good pastime. Music as a lifestyle is not healthy, but as a pastime within a lifestyle, it can be healthy.

I liked the mountains so much I ended up stayin' with the Whitleys that lived on Clarke's Creek Road near Valle Crucis. They needed help gettin' in their 'baccer crop and 'mater crop. It was payin' work. I decided to stay and help 'em get it all in. When the weather got cold, they started gradin' 'baccer, and I stayed on to learn how to do it. I went home right before Thanksgivin' and stayed until the next summer program started up again.

Durin' the second summer, I went round visitin' people I'd met the first year. I felt like I knew 'em and they knew me. There was a lot of enjoyment in sittin' round hearin' stories and learnin' ol' ballads and sech. I learned a lot of new tunes and got to watch how different ones picked the banjo.

STAYING ON

I knew I was gonna stay after the program was over. The Wilsons invited me to live with them, and they gave me work on their farm for a dollar an hour. I got to know a lot of people. The word spreads when there's a person who works hard in the field and doesn't mind helpin' out. I was thinkin' to leave when the 'baccer gradin' was over, but then I found out that after another month it would be time to get the 'baccer beds goin' for the next season. I stayed and helped people split wood and get it stacked for the winter.

I especially enjoyed visitin' Floyd and Dorsey Hicks and Floyd's sister, Hattie, and his mother, Buna. They had a daughter, Rosa Jane, close to my age. We became good friends. Floyd was the brother of Stanley Hicks— the most famous one in the family. He made banjos and performed all around the mountains, at the World's Fair, and won a lot of awards.

Nearly everyone in the Hicks family was talented to sing and play music. Both Stanley and Floyd learned to make banjos and delcimores [dulcimers] from their father and granddaddy. Since the Depression, they sold 'em to others. Floyd would get delcimores made so the Mast Store could sell 'em to tourists.

I got Floyd to make me a banjo—one that's usually called a fretless groundhog banjo. It was handmade from wood from his land. He cured the wood and shaped out the pieces. Sometime he tanned his own groundhog or muskrat to cover the sound hole.

After the next summer, I ended up buyin' my own trailer. The Smiths on Clarke's Creek Road had set up one trailer for their daughter on their property. They helped me set mine up and then I paid 'em twenty-five dollars a month—that included water and septic. I started doing all the work I could to support myself. First, different ones let me work in their fields, then they started knowin' me and kept askin' me to come for more work. I eventually helped Howell Cook and Rosa Jean's brother, Gordon Hicks, keep people in firewood. Then, I started sharecroppin' 'baccer with Howell.

Amy enjoyed leaning to play old mountain tunes on the banjo. Floyd Hicks built her a traditional fretless groundhog banjo. The Hicks family became famous for their knowledge of old stories, old music and for making delcimores [dulcimers] and banjos using local wood and animal hides. *Photograph courtesy of the Michels collection.*

Man Huntin'

In 1978, I was livin' in my little trailer and didn't have much land. That didn't stop me from wantin' a garden. I knew lots of people, and Maime Caudill was one of 'em. She didn't live too far away and I worked for her some. I met her when I lived with the Whitleys. Everyone called 'em Hubert and Mrs. Whitley, not Mr. and Mrs. Whitley.

Anyway, I used to ride over to Maime's to sell her cow milk, because Hubert and Mrs. Whitley milked a cow and didn't need all the milk. Early that summer, word got to me that Maime wanted me to garden with her. I said I would, especially knowin' that Maime was real ol' and needed help. I helped plant, hoe, weed and harvest in exchange for a share of the vegetables.

She lived by herself, but her grown children sometimes came to visit. I don't remember their names. The daughter didn't have much to say to me, but the son was always talkin' about religion.

One day I went over to work. To get to her house I had to walk up a long, narrow dirt road and turn back onto her dirt driveway up in the laurel thickets. I had just started up the drive and Maime's son and daughter were lyin' half hid in the laurel thicket, aimin' a gun out the drive.

That stopped me. I didn't think runnin' away would be too smart. So, I says, "Hallo there, what're ya huntin'?"

The brother said they were man huntin'. I could tell by then they'd had somethin' strong to drink. So, I asked, "Am I safe goin' up the driveway to the garden?"

He said, "Yeah, you're not a man."

So, I went on up the drive and worked in the garden. After that, I thought to be cautious as I walked up and down that road. I never found out what happened. When I finished my workin' and got my vegetables at the end of the summer, I never saw them again.

It came to me they musta took after their daddy. Somebody told me their daddy would get drunk and lie in the laurel thickets. When he was asked what he was doin', he'd say, "I'm layin' low."

THE SHULL SISTERS

I started rentin' a house from the Shull sisters all the way through gettin' married to Alfred. We were still in their house when our daughter, Dixie, was born. The house was bigger, so, I rented my trailer out. Wilhelmina ("Willy") and Anne were already pretty old. After I found out I was pregnant, I was visitin' in their house and I told Anne I was gonna have a baby. She said, "That's fine, as long as it doesn't get too big."

I had to laugh a little, but I knew it must be her hearin' aid wasn't workin' too well. I just thought I'd tell her again another day. A few days went by and I was back over to their house.

Anne said, "We heard at church that you're gonna have a baby. Why didn't you tell us?"

I laughed and told her that I did. She didn't know what I'd been sayin' to her that day. Her hearin' aid was off.

We had to take care of their yard as part of the house rent. Our yard ran together with what they considered their yard. It was big, with flowerbeds and hedges to trim. Also, when Willy and Anne went to Florida in the winter, I checked in on their brother, Don, to make sure he was okay.

When I moved in, they walked around with me and showed me which flowerbeds were for me to tend and which ones counted as theirs and were

The Shull sisters of Valle Crucis were kind landladies. Amy is shown (center) with them on their front porch in 1976. *Photograph courtesy of the Michels collection.*

part of the "rent" work. I think they did pay me a little for workin' in their flowerbeds.

It wasn't but a couple days later when I saw them over in what they told me was my flowerbeds, plantin' bulbs. I guessed they decided if they put 'em in my beds they could see 'em without payin' to keep 'em cleaned of weeds. I think they had plenty of money, but they were a little tight. In place of hot tea or coffee, they said they preferred to drink hot water. I just can't believe they really liked it better.

I planted a bed of ever-bearin' strawberries between their house and my garden, and told 'em they could pick what they wanted. One day when I was weedin' my corn, I saw Anne sneak out her back door. She looked one way and then the other way before she eased over to the strawberry bed. I didn't want to embarrass her and catch her at something that wasn't even wrong, so I just stayed down low till she got done pickin' and went to the house. For being in their late eighties they were in good shape and able to do a lot. Once I saw Anne out on her porch roof. It wasn't very steep, but it surprised me. She was washin' windows.

When Anne was about ninety, Dixie was old enough to run across the yard to visit them. Anne sat and held Dixie's hands and looked at her and said, "You're at one end of the road and I'm at the other end."

Amy joined the Roan Mountain Hilltoppers twenty-five years ago. They play old-timey mountain music. *Photograph courtesy of the Michels collection.*

THE HILLTOPPERS

After some time, different people heard me play and knew I liked the old tunes. Someone said I should meet Joe Birchfield at Roan Mountain. His family had a band called the Roan Mountain Hilltoppers. The Birchfield brothers, Joe and Creede, played way back before they had a band. They traveled pretty far, often by walkin' and carryin' their instruments. When Joe got married and had young'uns he put his fiddle down until his young'uns got up in age.

They got together as a band to play ol' traditional music with another brother, Ellick, and Joe's son, Bill. Janice married Bill and got everybody together as the Hilltoppers in 1975. Bill Ellick and Joe passed away and the band's continued with Bill and Janice.

I went over to meet 'em and play with 'em. For about a year after that, they'd call me if they needed somebody. Sometime I'd get a call just because Joe'd be mad at one of his brothers and he'd need me to take the place.

Twenty-five years have gone by and I still play with the Hilltoppers. The band has great timin'. They're famous for never having let their sound evolve into anything it's not. They keep the traditional music in the traditional manner, right to the T. It is one of the few string bands around with the old-time sound.

A lot of musicians want to do a lot of experimentin' and improvin'. That's not ole music. It's definitely not ole mountain music that has a washtub bass as one of its regular instruments. It's all about being handed down from one generation to the next and keepin' to the traditions that have come down to us.

The music started from the Birchfield family before the Civil War. Joe and Creede were born in a log house on Hampton Creek. Creede was born in 1905 and Joe in 1912. Their father was a farmer and blacksmith. It was their Uncle Johnny who liked to play the fiddle and taught 'em the music.

I play with Janice, Bill and Robbie Spencer. Some people want to know if there's still a traditional band out there. So many bands have gone modern; there are times I stand on stage and feel like a relic. But it feels good to bear the tradition of playin' music based on a way of life that's now gone. It's been handed down to me and to the others I perform with. It's a good feelin'. Not everybody can claim to have been this lucky.

I have always had an interest in the ole arts and ways of life. Any chance I have, I at least like to try doin' some of these lost arts.

Amy Michels

Natural Fixin's

In the spring I like gettin' out like the ole timers did and huntin' for the first green plants that sprout from the ground. I enjoy a meal of wilted branch lettuce along with fried 'taters flavored by ramps. It's important to pick the greens when they're young and tender. The lettuce can be eaten raw, just like the fancy greens that are popular, but I like it keeled.

People talk a lot about ramps. Actually, they look more like green onions, but they are best when they're small and young. If ya wait too long to pick 'em, they'll be tough. Some people pull a bunch and can 'em to use later. I like 'em best when they are fresh and I can get right home and fix 'em. Some people like to eat poke salad. I haven't gotten into that, however I reckon it's the same—ya got to pick it young and cook it fresh for the best flavor.

I was tellin' this to a neighbor one day. She said that restaurants in Boone pay big money to people diggin' large amounts of ramps, so they can pickle 'em. Neither of us ever heard of picklin' ramps. I tell everybody how good they are flavorin' eggs and 'taters, but I'm not sure it'd be the same after they'd be mixed in vinegar and spices.

Pickin' Berries

Every year I pick berries—blueberries, blackberries and black raspberries, mostly. But sometimes I find currants, gooseberries and red raspberries. I use 'em to make jam and freeze 'em for pies and sech in the winter. The best way to pick is to get a little half-gallon or one-gallon bucket with a handle and tie it around by sticking a belt through the handle and puttin' the belt on. A gallon milk jug with the top cut off works good. If a belt's not handy, then balin' twine works.

Then you have both hands free to hold back briars or branches to look while you pick. Sometimes my mind gets to wanderin' a lot, 'cause it don't take much thinking to pick berries. I'll be pickin' and wanderin' in my mind and droppin' the berries in my bucket, all while I look for the next ripe berries.

Then, I'll look down to see where I can step to. Once I realized a couple of big handfuls didn't land in the bucket. I had just turned loose of 'em without lookin' and they went on the ground.

This can make a body mad, frustrated and embarrassed all at the same time. It made me laugh at myself. I'm sure everybody that picks a lot of berries has done this. I'm pretty sure they do like me and look around to make sure nobody saw 'em do it.

IN AND OUT

Farmin' is a very important way of life. As long as all of the jobs are done, it leads to a cycle that makes a body satisfied and peaceful, and there's never really a chance to get bored. The jobs change with the seasons. Then they come back around in a familiar pattern. I think that's the ins and outs Ray Hicks used to tell of.

Seeds go *in* the ground, plants *up* and crops *out*. Then the vines and sech are plowed back *in*. Feed goes *in* the animals, manure *out* to the field and back *in* the ground. Trees come *out* of the woods. They're cut and brought *in* to burn or build with. Ashes go back *in* the ground. Mother plants are left *in* the ground to keep the cycle going.

This in and out has been goin' on season after season and year after year since the beginnin' of time. Not much is new, it keeps passin' generation to generation. Each mountain family taught their children how to survive and new generations keep comin' forth. There are just a few choices to be made of how the jobs get done.

By the time you get tired from one job, it's time for the next job: sow, hoe, harvest, can, make molasses, cut hay, clean stalls. Then, when you're wore out, it's winter: get firewood in—feedings are a little harder, but days are shorter—fix tools, mend. Then ya can rest. By the time you're tired of being rested, it's time to get seeds and start over again.

A LAVATORY BY ANOTHER NAME

What makes a day different is to get out doin' something, even if snow's on the ground and ya already fed the animals and brought in the wood. It's just as worthwhile to be able to help someone unexpectedly or visit someone that don't get much company. It's even better if there's time to stay awhile and hear a good 'n told. I hear good tales and try to think to write 'em down.

There is a little grocery store in the Smethport area called the Ashe Abattoir. Just for a store, especially in Ashe County, that's a kindly odd name. "Abattoir" is, I think, a French word that means, "where they butcher animals."

When we first come to Ashe County, they were still set up to butcher in that very same business out in the back part of the store. We took a few of our meat goats there before they closed out the butcherin'. But it's still called the Ashe Abattoir and sells gas and nabs and groceries.

The Michels grow much of their food. Alfred plows his fields with horses. *Photograph courtesy of the Michels collection.*

Feeding animals and cutting and hauling wood are non-stop activities on the farm. Alfred and Amy do a lot of wood splitting because they heat their home with wood and Amy cooks on a wood stove. *Photograph by B. Salsi.*

Ruth told me about her niece, Karen, gettin' a job at the Ashe "lavatory." I know she was talking about the Abattoir. I told a few people what Ruth said. They thought it was way funnier than I thought. I was thinkin' "lavatory" was a kind a sink.

So, I finally asked, "What is a lavatory? Now I know why it is right funny.

Treein' a Varmit

One evenin' when Alfred was gone, I was feedin' the animals. I got done and was walkin' from the barn toward the house. Polly, our dog, stopped and kept barkin' up a big pine tree. I was tryin' to get her to come on to the house, so I stopped to look to see if there was somethin' up in the tree.

I was pretty sure it'd be a squirrel or some sort of bird flutterin' around in the branches. I didn't have my glasses on and was about to give up lookin' when I realized there was a coon settin' on the lowest set of branches. It coulda jumped on me for how close it was.

So, I thought, "Okay, that's what's been gettin' my ducks."

I wasn't sure what to do. I expected Alfred home soon. I considered standin' there keepin' it treed 'til he got home. By then, it was a little after 5:00 p.m. So, on a chance he was already at the house, I started hollerin' and whistlin' real loud. Then I kept hollerin', "Help!"

It got to where my throat was givin' out, and the coon chattered back at me like he was fussin' every time I hollered. I really knew it was a far stretch to expect anyone to hear me. About 5:15, I realized no one was comin' and it was gonna get dark—and without my glasses I'd lose the coon. Without a flashlight, I couldn't keep it treed. So, I started sightin' up my finger, first one eye, then the other, then both eyes to figure out which was my gun eye. All this time, the coon was chatterin' back at my sightin'. I figured out my left eye was my sightin' eye. I told Polly to stay.

I knew she wouldn't, and she didn't. I ran on down to the house with Polly runnin' after me. I got my shotgun, a shell, my glasses and the cordless phone. While I was headin' out the door, I put my glasses on. Then, I loaded the gun and set the hammer. Next, I dialed my neighbor's number, still thinkin' I might keep the coon treed if it was still there. I'd like to get Ivan over to shoot it. By the time I got the number dialed, I was near the pine tree and there sat the coon just lookin' at me. It had come out of the tree and was settin' at the base. We were lookin' at each other. I knew I was about to lose my chance to get the coon, so I threw the phone down on the ground, sighted with my left eye, took time aim and KABOOM. I got it!

Then, I thought, "Oh, Lordy. I've dialed the neighbor's number."

She'd picked up the phone and heard the KABOOM.

So, I redialed and told her the whole story. She started repeatin' what I said sentence by sentence to her husband. She knew Alfred wasn't wantin' to eat coon.

She said, "Now, you can skin it out, stretch the hide on a board and have a big pot of water boilin' when Alfred comes in. Then tell him you hunted him a coon."

Just a few days before this, a feller over on Silas Creek got his picture in the paper with a four-hundred-and-fifty-pound bear he'd killed. So I said, "I'm gonna have my picture made holdin' the coon up by the tail and have it put in the paper."

My neighbor said, "Yeah, they can show it and say 'Amy's first coon.'"

I told her I might get to likin' it and quit everythin' else to go huntin' all the time.

Needin' a Cat

There are not many times in an adult's life when one actually says, "I want to get a cat." When one does, it's not so much, "Where will I find one?" as it is, "Which one will I get?" Once you announce you want a cat, everyone will tell ya they know where ya can get free cats for the takin'—and gladly. The last time Alfred said, "I need a cat for the barn," a three-ring circus was set in motion.

We started by gettin' a grown orange female that'd been spayed. I was anxious to let it out. When I got home, I opened the cage and let it go. My other cat, Cali Bob, and my dog came over. When my old cat saw the new cat, he jumped at it. Then he and my dog, Leroy, chased it off into the woods.

I tried to go out and find it to bring it back, but I never found it. I still had the cat cage, so after several days, Alfred said again, "I need a cat for the barn."

Cali Bob was gettin' too ole to care about keepin' the mice problem down. Alfred said, "Should we go to town to get one at the pound?"

I said, "No, you don't have to go that far. I think I can get a cat and be back home quicker than I could get to town."

So, I called down to Flap's Store, half a mile down the road. I said, "Flap, I need a cat."

He said, "Come on to the store, there's plenty here."

I took the cat cage and went down. His cats were mostly wild. People dumped 'em off at his store and he fed 'em. They stayed, but nobody could get near most of 'em. That's perfect for a barn cat—not easy to catch and a little wild.

Flap opened a can of cat food and a can of dog food and set the cans on the woodstove, which was hot. He said he'd bait the cage with that. He said, "The smell draws 'em best when the food's warm. They can smell it better."

He left me in charge of the store while he went home to get leather gloves. When he came back, he put the food in the cage outside. I waited in the store and about five seconds later he came back in and said he'd got a cat. "I got the one I call Chub," he said.

Then, he held up his arm and said, "What do you do for scratches?"

The cat left one long scratch bleedin' up his arm and a smaller scratch on the other side. Flap said, "Alcohol—that's what I use."

So, while he was doctorin' his arm, I went on home with my new cat. I didn't want to lose this one. I fixed up my big doodle cage in the barn loft and put the cat cage in it, so Chub would have more room. She lived in there about five days. When I put food in the cage, she wouldn't get near me.

Leroy and Chub got nose to nose through the wire, so I left the chicken cage open. She finally got out when I wasn't watchin'. She'd sit and watch me and meow, but she wouldn't let me come near her.

Chub ended up havin' three kittens. I finally got her tame enough to where I could touch her, but by then she had hidden her kittens. When they were runnin' around I couldn't catch them. So, I got to thinkin'— which was worse, a barn full of rats and mice or a barn full of cats?

When the kittens got up in size, we had four barn cats. One day, the dogs were barkin' and jumpin' around up in the barn. I went to see what had got in the barn. Chub was all tore up. When I looked up, I saw a kitten was caught in a gap between the floorin' and the sidin' of the barn loft. It was hangin' by its neck and squallin'. But, it at least had its hind feet on a brace. I tried to pull it up and couldn't. Then, I tried to pull it down. That didn't work either. I took a hammer and tried to knock the wall back. I thought about that and decided the noise might make the kitten go deaf. I went down and got a wreckin' bar. I wedged it in real good and pulled as hard as I could. The kitten dropped all the way down before I could get my hands on it.

I went downstairs and there it sat on a two-by-four, too stunned to move. Alfred had a customer in his fiddle shop. When I asked him to take the cat, he said he would. So that made three cats. Shortly after that, someone we knew was askin' about a cat, and that's when Chub got a new home. We were down to two barn cats.

I spent a long time playin' with those two—with a cane stalk or anything long. Then I worked my way closer and closer to 'em, 'til I could kindly catch them. I got feelin' sorry for 'em and decided to have 'em fixed so they could keep each other company. Lucky I did; they're both girls. They're still in the barn—an orange cat and a Siamese-lookin' one. Their names are Possum and Blossom.

We don't have mice in the barn anymore, so I don't know if we'll ever again say, "I think we need a cat."

PIG'S PIG

After work one day I turned the car to go up our steep driveway and there stood a hog lookin' at me like I'd upset his plans. He walked on up the driveway. I drove partway up and parked by Alfred's fiddle shop, which isn't far from the road. I got out wonderin' what to do with the hog, 'cause I didn't want it to go in my garden.

Alfred was in the shop with his apprentice, Alex. I heard one of 'em holler somethin' about a huge dog. Then, they were out there with me. We decided it probably belonged to Pig Price, about a mile up the road.

So Alex and me each got a stick, and with my dog, Polly, we drove it down the driveway and started up the road. Clyde, our neighbor, was settin' on the porch of a little building he has out by the road. He was watchin' to see what would happen, 'cause he had run the hog out of his yard not long before it come to our place. He said it probably was Pig Price's hog, for Pig had been on a week-long drunk and his hog had been wanderin' in the woods all that time.

Alex and Polly and I kept on a leadin' that hog up the road. A couple of cars passed. Everybody in the cars seemed extra smiley and happy. We got to Pig's trailer, but nobody was home. We looked around and saw the hog lot. It was on the other side of the creek, with a good bridge close by. We started drivin' the hog to the bridge, but his mind was workin' different than ours right then. He decided to go down in the creek and turn downstream under the bridge, through a water gate and into a pasture with the cattle, instead of upstream to his hog lot.

The fields were real wet and nasty. After about five or ten minutes of tryin' to turn the hog around with not much luck, we decided he was close enough to his home and gave up. We got back down the road a little piece and looked back. What we saw was a long line of cows walkin' a path with a large hog right behind 'em. I don't know if the cows were tryin' to get away from the hog or if the hog decided to join the cows, but I think they were all well used to each other. We gave up and left them to work it out on their own.

SOUTHERN HOSPITALITY

Southern hospitality is a common-enough phrase. Some people might not even think about what it really means, but I think it can have different meanings. Bob Harmon was a fine example of real mountain-style southern hospitality. He probably doesn't know it. One summer I helped a neighbor paint the trim on her house. Then, Bob hired me to paint his garage and work shed and storage shed. I spent quite a few days there. He already knew my family and me, but not well. I figured we kinda became friends while I was paintin', for he was there the whole time.

About half a year later, Alfred ended up repairin' a fiddle that had a metal tailpiece painted red. Well, the owner wanted it to be black. In place of buyin' a whole can of metal spray paint, which we might never need again, I said, "I'd take it to Bob Harmon."

I knew he had the right kind of paint, so that's what I did. I didn't realize that durin' that half a year, Bob had been sick and suffered a little memory loss. Well, I knocked on his door. He opened it, and me not always thinkin' of good manners first, I said, "Howdy. I come to ask a favor of you."

He said, "What is it?" I showed him the tailpiece and told him we needed it painted black. He said he'd get his shoes on. So he did, and I followed him around the house to the backyard where his work shed is. Partway around, he turned and looked at me and said, "Do I know you?"

It surprised me, but I explained who I was. He remembered and went on and painted the tailpiece for me.

I have thought about that every now and again. In a way, I guess it was almost like going to a complete stranger's house askin' for a favor.

How many places can a person go and have a favor so easily and willingly done? Maybe anywhere in this country, if you get lucky and choose the right person—but if you do, I'd say they've got a fine dose of Southern hospitality inside 'em.

FARM LIVIN' MIGHT NOT BE FOR CITY PEOPLE

Sometimes I get so use to livin' on the farm with farm neighbors, I tend to forget not everyone lives like this. Some, maybe lots of people, have different ways about 'em. We had a friend visit us here from Pennsylvania. She seemed to love farms, so I overlooked the fact she really didn't live on one nor did she know farm ways.

While she was here, I offered her use of my washin' machine to wash her clothes. She got her clothes started, and then got busy and forgot to take 'em out. I did it for her, and hung 'em on the clothesline out on the front porch.

Later she came in the front door right past her clothes hangin' there and looked in the washin' machine. She asked, "Where are my clothes?"

I said, "They're dryin'."

We happened to have a freezer about the size of a dryer out in the hallway. She went there and opened the freezer, thinkin' it was a dryer. She realized her mistake and said, "Where is the dryer?"

I didn't bother explainin' I had a piece of line strung across the porch and I used that for a dryer. I just said, "On the porch."

She looked on the back porch—no dryer. By now my daughter, Dixie, was standin' there watchin' her like she couldn't believe what was happenin'.

I said, "Look on the front porch."

Southern hospitality extends to an annual molasses boiling at Alfred and Amy's. They grow, harvest and crush cane. Helpers get a taste of molasses and experience a day on the farm. *Photograph courtesy of the Michels collection.*

She did, but she was still looking for an electric dryer, and still didn't notice her clothes a hangin' there. I finally had to go out and show her.

VISITIN' THE HICKS

Durin' some of the time I spent with Gordon Hicks in the seventies and eighties, we rode around in his truck and visited his people. Ray Hicks was his cousin on his daddy's—Floyd Hicks's—side. Ray's wife, Rosie, was his aunt on his mama's—Dorsey Harmon's—side. Sometimes we stopped by to visit Ray and Rosie.

I learned by Gordon's example the natural way to visit in their part of the country. For one, you don't need to take 'em nothin', but it's nice to have chewin' 'baccer or smokes to offer out of your pouch or pack. If they offer you to eat a bite with 'em, it's best to do it whether you're hungry or not; it makes 'em happy to be able to feed you.

It's best to let 'em start and carry the conversations the way they want 'em to go. They might be slow to get started. They might ask how others you both know are gettin' along. Then they might ask what they've been doin'. Then if they move on to other subjects of their own it's helpful.

Ray and Rosie would both start together with the talkin'. Soon Ray would carry it. He usually talked about life events in his past and his family's past. Then he'd sing a few songs, ole ones, before he goes on to some sort of ole Jack tale or sech.

With Gordon there I got used to a certain easy, natural way of response, which flowed nicely back and forth. The response was an expression and obvious interest, more than a vocal response.

I knew Ray did shows at festivals and other public performances, but I'd never seen that for myself. Then, in the fall of 1998, and again in 1999, he told the tale of "Hardy Hardhead" at a festival where our group was playin' music.

I had just gone to visit him and Rosie a few weeks before that, and he had told me the same tale. I think now, he was tellin' it to me to practice and make sure he remembered it well enough. Of course, he always tells a few details different, but some things need to stay in a certain order. Then, as I listened to him tell it to an audience, I saw things in a different light.

This audience didn't really know how he lived, and they were all used to a very different way of life. The gesturin' Ray used, which seems natural and normal for him in his own house, seems exaggerated in a different settin'. I could tell the listeners were tickled over it, but they

When Amy moved to the Blue Ridge Mountains, she enjoyed visiting many of the people who traced their history back over a hundred years. That's when Ray Hicks was developing his reputation as a master storyteller. Ray's house became the mecca of storytelling in North Carolina. *Photograph by Amy Michels.*

didn't understand it for what it really meant, and I almost felt like they were laughin' at him, inside themselves. It didn't make me feel good. I wished they understood, but also realized they didn't—and maybe couldn't. They had nothin' in their lives to compare it to.

Also, Ray's choice of words and ways of pronouncin' them sounded natural at his house, but his ole way of talkin' had the same effect on the crowd as his gesturin'. My heart was hurt to think he was being made fun of, and him knowin' everything 'bout mountain stories and the ole ways of livin'. We were given twenty minutes for our music, twenty minutes for Ray, so much time to eat, twenty minutes for us and twenty minutes for Ray.

People have been "trained" to accept time schedules. There is time to go to work, time to quit work, time of TV shows, even commercials—everything to a schedule. People have forgotten how to concentrate past a certain amount of time without an "intermission" or interruption. This is not so with the ole ways—get up with daybreak (which changes with the seasons), work 'til the job's done and tell a story 'til it's done.

Well, the festival people interrupted Ray's story in the middle to fit the time slot they had for him. That really ruined his story, 'cause he had to

Amy captured Ray Hicks mid-story as he told her a Jack tale circa 1979. Amy's string band sometimes played at a festival where Ray performed. His southern Appalachian dialect was part of his storytelling trademark. *Photograph by Amy Michels.*

take time to get warmed up to it and get himself into it again. He was flustered and wanted to finish when they stopped him. He says, "I'm just a-gettin' to the good part." But they wouldn't let him continue. Ray told Rosie to remember what part he was at so he could start back.

Durin' the dinner break, some of the audience was discussin' that they couldn't understand Ray, but they were really enjoyin' him. He is to be enjoyed, but I think they were missin' so much—they just couldn't see. They looked over and asked me if I could understand him. I wasn't expectin' to have to discuss Ray with them.

I admitted I couldn't always hear Ray, but that I was used to the words he used, so that wasn't a problem. I guess they figured if somebody doesn't talk like them they don't understand it. I hope I made them realize it's not really like that. I admired Ray for being able to get out among so many types of peoples and places and still not lose who he was. He was happy and satisfied with the life and people he was raised a part of.

POLECAT CROSSIN'

Carolyn Cannon and me graded 'baccer together one fall. She and her husband, Wayne, had rented use of the barn behind our house to hang 'baccer in that year. Men in a farmin' family had a way of makin' themselves scarce if their work didn't involve trucks or tractors, so Carolyn was gradin' 'baccer and I helped some.

Her young'uns were almost as ole as me, but I always did get on better with older people. We got to talkin' about this, that, everything and nothin' like you do when you're workin' long hours together.

Somehow we brought up the subject of how there were so many polecats between the Mast Store and Frank Baird's house, or at least we smelled 'em there a lot. We saw 'em dead and alive on the road. In our talk, we decided there should be a polecat crossin' sign.

It was funny to think about it. Later on in the week, I made up my mind to make the sign. I wanted Carolyn in on it, but too many times if you don't do somethin' on your own, it don't get done.

On the weekend, after dark, I had Alfred drive me out to where I wanted to put the sign up. He didn't want to, but he did anyway. He let me out and I told him to drive up the road, then come back and get me, so my truck wouldn't be seen and I wouldn't get caught. I don't know why I was scared of gettin' caught, but that's part of the story.

I picked a bad night, 'cause a dance was lettin' out at the Apple Barn and there were more cars out than usual. There I was tryin' to post the sign with me not gettin' seen on the road, but I got it done and got on back home.

A couple of days later, Carolyn told me her family went on a horse-and-buggy ride and saw the sign. When she saw it, she knew it was me and got a bigger tickle than anyone, since she was in on the plannin'.

The next day I was in the Mast Store buyin' somethin' and the conversation at the counter turned toward the sign. I still wasn't lettin' on I did it. I was real interested in hearin' what they had to say, though. Devry Mast thought it was funny. Then, Frank Baird's sister thought it was funny. Finally, I fessed up to doin' it.

A day or two later the sign was gone. I guess somebody liked it good enough to take it. But I think it shoulda been left up for a little bright spot in an ordinary day.

THE DUMPIN' TRUCK

I won't never forget the day I ran over Alfred with a dumpin' truck. We had been haulin' gravel, gettin' started buildin' our cabin. To haul it, we borrowed a neighbor's dumpin' truck. It didn't work quite right, so before the bed would raise, a person had to crawl under the truck and adjust some of the works by hand.

Well, Alfred had dumped most of the gravel and had a little left. He drove a little way down the driveway and decided on a good spot to dump the rest. So there he was, under the truck, with his legs stickin' out by the back dual wheels. I looked and happened to notice the truck roll a little. I said for him to be careful, for the truck just moved. He told me to climb in and mash the brake. Then he said, "Be sure not to touch the clutch." Anyone that has driven a straight drive knows when you get behind the wheel, your automatic reaction is to pop the clutch.

I ended up gettin' confused and popped the clutch after all. The truck rolled a little. Alfred's overall legs got caught and he said, "Crank it up and back up."

Well, I'd never driven a dumpin' truck and it's not easy in a straight drive to back up on a steep hill without it rollin' forward a little first. I was tryin' so hard I killed the motor twice or so, and Alfred a hollerin' the whole time. I was runnin' over him. I was killin' him. I was gettin' so nervous my legs was shakin' and I couldn't work the pedals right. I tried again, and Alfred seemed to calm down.

He said I could quit now, I'd done run over him. His overalls and shirt were torn up pretty bad and his leg was bruised and scraped, but that was all. I called a first responder and asked what to do for bruises. I was too shaken up to tell how bad they were or what caused 'em. All he needed was aspirin to keep the blood thinned and from clottin'. I kept calendula salve on his leg, bound with a comfrey leaf. Then that was held on with an Ace bandage.

Marriage Is Dangerous

After news got out about this, we heard about another close call, provin' how dangerous it can be to be married.

There was a man who wanted to clean his chimney, but his roof was steeply pitched. He decided he'd feel safer with somethin' to hold on to. He got a long length of rope and tied one end to the bumper of his truck. He somehow got the rope slung across the roof of the house and went up the other side with the rope to hold on to.

While he was up there, his wife took a sudden notion she had to go somewhere. Without knowing where her husband was, she ran out to the truck, jumped in and took off. Well, her husband had tied his end of that rope around his waist. When the truck went, so did he. I'm not sure how far they got before his wife realized she was draggin' her husband down the road.

And, then, there's always the party-line effect of a story. By the time it gets back around to the beginnin', it's not the same story. Whenever I ran over Alfred, it wasn't but a day or two later, our next-door neighbors said they heard Frank broke his leg over here.

I figured it was Frank's truck and Alfred's bruised legs. Frank wasn't even at our house that day.

Oh, No. Not Again!

We didn't learn our lesson very well about borrowin' the dumpin' truck, so we got smart and borrowed it again.

This time Frank was doin' the drivin'. We were movin' dirt. We had some left over and we knew where we could put it. There's a small section of our creek where we had put a culvert, and we were buildin' the ground up over it. To get the truck backed up to it, the truck was at an angle. That put the passenger side on the down side of the hill and the driver's side on the upper end. Alfred got under and adjusted the works some. The bed went up a little, but not enough, so Alfred was tryin' to work with it with a long stick. Meanwhile, all the dirt shifted to the lower side of the truck, which was where Alfred was standin'.

I saw the truck gettin' thrown off balance and hollered to Alfred to get out of the truck. Alfred moved, but Frank stayed put. It was almost like in slow motion. The truck slowly rolled over and landed where Alfred had been standin'. It landed on the passenger side. After all the crashing quieted down, I said, "Frank, are you okay?"

Real slow and quiet-like, he says, "I think I swallered my cigar."

We had some other equipment here workin' on the house site and they came down and turned the dumpin' truck back right side. All they had to do was beat a few dents out and put more water in the radiator and the truck was fine. I told Frank to take that truck home. I didn't want to ever see it here again.

Talkin' English—Gettin' the Words Right

Different words become accepted and used by different people all across the country. It depends on where people live and what is said in each community. I think it is only right to accept the fact that country people have their own words, which may not be ol' words or the right words, but they are used and accepted within a certain area of people. That's all a word is—it's a sound to let others know what you want to tell them. If they know what you're talking about, it's served its purpose.

Bill says an ol'-time banjo has a "resignator." We know it has a "resonator."

Bill's granddaughter, Samantha, was with us after we played a set at the Roan Mountain Rhododendron Festival. Her mama, Debbie, bought her and Rachel some sort of animal toy on a bouncy wire handle. I asked Samantha what kind of animal it was. She said it was a "crack-a-daughter." I looked at it again and realized it looked like a crocodile.

If a person tells somethin' to Bill that he thinks is right, he will let you know he "consumes so."

Bill showed me two fiddles he made. One had a dark brown fingerboard. I asked what kind of wood it was. He said, "Warnut." I've heard Ruth say "warnut" a lot, too. There are new words added to the American language all the time.

Bill Birchfield says "corgation" for "coordination," but the old-timers said, "corgagation." Janice's comment to that, "Oh, Bill. The ole-timers didn't even know that word."

Janice says Bill is crazier than a "runned over rat."

Bill used to work at the Levi plant. He says he inspected the goods as they come down the "surveyor" belt.

If the odds of somethin' are bad, ask Bill. "Ten chances out of nine, it won't work."
Ask Bill if your instrument sounds in tune. He'll listen and tell you at least one string is a "fracture" off.

C.M. "Stimmy" Putnam picks guitar some with the Hilltoppers. The word "confused" came up. He allows as how the "fuse" isn't so bad, it's the "corn" that'll get ya.

"JOB'S TURKEY"

Bill and Janice and me was settin' around with a friend of theirs, Penny. Now, Penny is very fond of another friend, Steve. Bill was tellin' Penny how Steve is awful set in his ways, since he's been a bachelor for so long, and it would take "the patience of Job's ole turkey hen" to get along with him for any length of time. Now, I've heard that expression before, and didn't think about it, but Penny had never heard it. She repeated it, includin' an exclamation mark.

Janice laughed and said it's really "the patience of Job," but Bill's family always said "Job's old turkey hen." They live in and have always lived in Roan Mountain, Tennessee, way over in Carter County, at least sixty-five miles away over the mountains. It got me to studyin' how did it get spread around. Some phrases and words are so ole they've been brought over with the first immigrants that settled the mountains. Is this one of those phrases? I really don't think so. Modern phrases are spread around on TV, radio

Flap's Store is a community gathering place. Amy says Flap is a good one to tell a story. Here she is shown with Flap Allen. *Photograph by B. Salsi.*

The Michels built their house from trees they felled on their land. It is an efficient log cabin with few modern amenities. Amy says, "We don't like fancy." *Photograph by B. Salsi.*

and newspapers so that surely doesn't apply. Then I wondered if some ole country preacher got up all excited at a revival and said it once. For country folk did tend to listen to what was said to them at these emotionally charged meetin's. For whatever reason, the patience of "Job's old turkey hen" is here to stay.

HAPPY DAY

Hattie and me were workin' in the greenhouse and went out for a break. Her job was done, and she said, "I wonder what in the happy I'll be doin' next?"

I didn't quite catch that one, so asked her about it. Now, Hattie isn't one for bad language. She allows as how everyone else uses the "H" word, so that's her "H" word.

Evelyn Gentry tells about a guitar picker she knows. He tried another feller's guitar, and declared, "The strings are too close apart."

Hattie tells of a young man sent out from the agriculture office to check their 'baccer field. He had on fancy cowboy boots. After he walked across the field, she says he pulled out his "hanchacuff" to wipe the mud off his boots.

I went to the hardware store for some slidin'-barn-door parts. The man what waited on me got carried away talkin' about long ago "mollasy boilin's" and makin' cider and music events. He told me about a woman at a fiddlers' convention. He said people were dancin' all around the stage, and she got up there dancin' with barely enough clothes on "fer a gnat a hanchacoof."

RECIPE

I gave Hattie some pears at work one day, and she told me she had a good pear preserve recipe. I said, "What is it?"
She said, "I make it with pears, pineapple and mozzarella cherries."

I took some raspberries I'd picked to my neighbor, Ruth Lewis. She said they'd just robbed their bees and asked if I wanted a quart of honey. She also said she had a good "restapee" usin' honey in a ham glaze.

DESCRIBIN' THINGS

Some ways of describin' things around the mountains brings ya right back where you started, sech as in decidin' somethin'. It's "six to one, half dozen to the other." Or, in choosin' a road to take, "one's just as broad as it is long." That means either road is okay.

I stopped at Harold's Shoes outside of Boone one day, and this note was on the door:

Be Back
In 30: -mi
Sary I missted
You

He never said what time he left, so I couldn't tell when the thirty minutes were up.

I stopped at Flap Allen's store for a cabbage head. He had a sign posted on the door:

"a helifer for sale and Nubian goats."

Another sign was announcing someone was buyin' cows:

"old cows, slow cows, cull cows, bull cows."

Editor's note:
Amy Michels and her husband, Alfred, live as old-timey as possible, except they do have electricity. Otherwise Amy cans, cooks on a wood stove, makes quilts out of scraps, recycles, helps her neighbors, raises chickens and ducks and is one of the most accommodating people I've ever known.

Alfred builds fine string instruments. He plows the old way, ball-hoots trees off the mountain and together with Amy they grow their eatin', harvest and chop firewood. They grind cane to make molasses and raise cows and horses. Both are talented musicians and have played with many award-winning bands.

The Michels believe in simplicity in their surroundings and stay true to farm values. They built their log house from trees on their land. Many students from Appalachian State University in Boone apprentice with Alfred Michels. He presents them with a living history experience and also teaches them how to build fine fiddles, basses and cellos.

Amy retains a specific southern mountain dialect. She rarely puts "g" on "ing" words and there are times when she adds "in" to words that don't require it, as in "dumpin" truck, rather than "dump" truck. She always says "sech" for "such," "idée" for idea." Many have heard of the song "Boil them Cabbage Down." To Amy and other mountain people it's "bile." As for her husband, Alfred, he's from Germany and retains a German accent with no hint of southern Appalachian. However, he knows the Southern dialectical words to hundreds of old mountain music tunes.

GLENN BOLICK

SAWMILL MAN, POTTER, SINGER AND SONGWRITER

I was the sixth child born at home. The woman doctor, Dr. Warfield, came from Blowing Rock to be with Mama. The doctor later opened a little clinic in Blowing Rock. Mama went there for her other four children to be born.

SETTLIN' THE BLUE RIDGE

Our farm was in Caldwell County, within a stone's throw of the Watauga County line. I could see it up yonder at the top of the mountain. My great-great-grandfather, Abner Bolick, and his brothers came from Germany to settle in Catawba County near Hickory, North Carolina. Then, Abner drove his cattle up the John's River to the Upton community in Globe Valley to graze in the summer. He liked it so much he decided to move his family there if the cattle could survive the winter.

The next spring, Abner moved his wife to the area. They built a log house and raised a large family. My great-grandfather, Marcus Bolick, was Abner's son. He married Susan Green. They moved to the Bailey's Camp community when he got fifty acres from his father-in-law. Later Marcus and Susan inherited another two hundred acres from the Green side of the family. Bailey's Camp was named for the hunter John Bailey. He set up a camp where he butchered and salted game to preserve it. He was there around 1790. Sometimes later in the 1800s, my great-great-grandfather Green purchased the land.

I was born to the old ways of farming in the valley to help our family keep food on the table. My early experiences included sawmilling. When I was old enough to tote water buckets for my father's sawmill crew, I was out in the woods with 'em. Life was not too bad. We had enough to eat, which was better than a lot of people. We had a lot of love from our grandparents. Since I wasn't the oldest or the youngest, I shared the work with older brothers and had younger brothers to pass some off to.

Going to Church

My family was religious. We didn't miss a Sunday at church—nor a prayer meeting, revival or association meeting. It was always to be remembered that my great-grandfather, a devout German Lutheran, helped organize the first church in the area. The closest Lutheran church was forty miles away. That was a long horse-drawn or mule-drawn wagon ride to have a child baptized. My family couldn't travel that far regularly; it had to be a special occasion or a special revival meeting.

The first Lutheran meetings close to our valley took place when the first preachers came for a camp meeting and lived in tents pitched near Great-granddaddy Mark's house. The women met and prepared food for everybody in a mud rock furnace. The children assembled beside Great-granddaddy's porch to sing hymns and give camp yells.

By the time the Lutheran church was built on the ridge in 1926, Great-granddaddy was almost eighty years old. He had given my grandfather, Jethro, part of his land. Granddaddy furnished the land for the church. The wood was given by my great-granddaddy from trees cut on his property. Members named the church St. Mark's Evangelical Lutheran Church to honor my great-grandfather Marcus, whom everyone called "Mark."

Cora Pearl Jeffcoat, the daughter of the first regular minister, Reverend H.W. Jeffcoat, wrote in the *Lutheran Magazine*, "Marcus Bolick kept the fire of Lutheranism alive." The church is still standing. I drive by it every time I come and go from my house.

When my father married my mother, her dad was not pleased. This caused my parents to join a little Baptist church near our house. Needless to say, my brothers and sisters and I were brought up in both churches. We were back and forth depending on which was having a service, funeral, revival or Bible school. I sometimes look back and think I had a double-dose of preaching and hymn singing.

Papa usually had a pickup truck to use in his business and also for the family. The back had wooden sideboards. He and Mama rode up front with the littlest young'uns. The rest of us stood in the back and held on to the sides.

My biggest memories of preaching were the revivals that could go on every night for two weeks. When I was little, the preaching scared me. The preacher would get loud and get on the devil. He'd pace back and forth and lean over toward the congregation to make his points. The Bolick young'uns had to be reverent no matter what. My parents wouldn't allow us to lie down on the bench and go to sleep like some of the other young'uns. Sitting through those services when I was four, five and six years was near torture.

When I was eight and nine, I got scared the devil would get me. I could understand better what was being said. The preacher would get on talking about us going to hell. That bothered me a lot. I knew I didn't want to go there.

By the time I was fourteen, I got more appreciation for the revival experience. Some of the preachers were memorable characters. Reverend Roe Payne was my favorite. He wore his long-sleeved shirt with garters to hold up his sleeves. He'd say, "Let's have a little fellowship and strike hands one with another." I liked to hear him speak. He could keep our attention.

FARMIN' THE VALLEY

I grew up not knowing much about what my father did, but I saw what Mama did. Although Papa was a good provider by furnishing us with food, shoes and clothes, he expected his young'uns to work hard. We heated our house and Mama's cook stove with wood. Papa had a team of horses pull a whole tree into the yard. It was up to the boys to get out and cut up the wood and carry it in. We'd cut up the limbs and trunk and everything. When we saw it coming, we knew what we'd be doing after school all the next week.

Our large garden fed our family. With Papa out sawmilling most of the week, it fell to Mama and the young'uns to do most of the garden work. It had to be fenced in to keep the cattle out, but there wasn't a space inside that fence left unplanted.

Then, there were our three cows that had to be milked twice a day. Lester, Boyd and I took care of that before school and then before dark every day for years. It was miserable getting out on cold mornings. But they had to be fed twice a day, except in summer when we'd feed 'em once a day and they'd get out and eat grass.

Glenn's Uncle Rufus is standing in front of his log cabin with his wife, Mary Holler Bolick (center), and their neighbor, Nancy Ann Crump. *Photograph courtesy of the Bolick family collection.*

Mama oversaw all of the work we did. She ran the farm and got us out working plowing, planting, hoeing, harvesting and caring for animals. We carried in the harvest and my mother and my sisters canned everything to put in the can house to see us through the winter. We grew just about everything we ate and it was up to Mama to figure out how it should be kept so we didn't go hungry.

When apples were ripe, the whole family helped pick the fruit and haul it to the house. Then we all sat around peeling and peeling. Mama canned apple butter, apple jelly and applesauce. When all that was done, she let the young'uns grind up apples for fun to get cider.

Some sort of fruit was ripe for months. We had early apples to come in June. Then, different kinds of apples ripened in the summer and others came in the fall. We had fresh apples five months of the year— from June until frost in late October. About once a month, Mama made us a batch of sugar cookies. Our favorite was what she called her "knee-deep apple cake." She'd use cookie dough and spread apples between ten or twelve layers of the dough. That tall apple cookie cake was something to see for a few seconds, because that's how long it lasted.

We also had pears, plums and mountain peaches. The peaches were small, but delicious—sweet as sugar. Mama usually got enough to make a few jars of peach preserves.

St. Mark's Church was named for Glenn's great-grandfather. He is attributed with keeping Lutheranism alive in the community. *Photograph by B.Salsi.*

We had pumpkins, early June peas, cabbage, beans, cucumbers, 'maters, corn, beets, carrots, turnips, squash, 'taters and grape vines. Papa would trade several bushels of Irish 'taters for bushels of sweet taters. He'd trade for things we couldn't grow. Mama made stewed 'maters and put away jars of juice. She used the grapes for grape jelly and grape juice. We put whole pumpkins under haystacks out in the field to keep 'em from freezin'.

Then we could go out, even with snow on the ground, and find the pumpkins for Mama to make a pumpkin pie or pumpkin mush. Before the first frost, Mama might get eight or ten pumpkins canned and in the can house. The others were the ones that went under the hay. We took the leftover seeds and fiber and mixed it with the cow feed. When Granddaddy had extra pumpkins, he chopped the things up and fed his cows.

My parents and grandparents didn't hold to many superstitions, but my granddaddies held to the almanac for planting and butchering. They wouldn't butcher unless they consulted the almanac. They wouldn't butcher on a full moon, either. If they killed on the full moon, they said the meat would roll up in the pan.

Papa and Mama read the almanac and tried to be close to what it said, but they didn't hold to everything. Papa usually butchered hogs the Saturday after Thanksgiving. The weather had to be right. If it was too warm, he'd put it off. When he did butcher, he'd get help cuttin' them up from a relative or one of his crew. They'd haul the meat up to our apple house. Then he'd leave it all there for Mama to take care of.

My brothers and I helped her set up boards to lay the meat on. She'd pour salt on the boards and then she'd salt both sides of the meat. After the meat took the salt, we'd hang it up in the meat house to dry and cure for later eating. Some people would holler out a log and lay the hams down in the log poured full of salt. That made the hams too salty for my taste, but many did it as a way to protect the meat from wild animals.

Mama took an axe and chopped open the head. She'd take the brains out and use them for cooking brains and eggs for breakfast. She'd clean the hair off the head and take all the meat she could off the bone to use to mix with the liver to make liver mush. We'd get out the hand-turned meat grinder and make sausage by mixing spices in with lean trimming and some fat trimming. She pulled the fat off the guts and then cooked it with the other fat and render out lard. She poured it in jars. The leftover little fried-up fat pieces were called "cracklin's." It made the best cracklin' cornbread; it'd make a hound dog break his chain.

She saved the lard in the can house in gallon jars. When it was time to eat the meat, she might soak it in a little vinegar and water to get some of the

The Bolicks, staunch Lutherans, came from Germany and settled in the Blue Ridge Mountains. Great-granddaddy Mark hosted camp meetings and revivals on his land in the late 1800s. The photo shows members of a Western North Carolina church after a revival meeting in 1895. *Photograph courtesy of the North Carolina Office of Archives and History.*

salt out. Mama didn't waste a thing. She fried the meat skin and we loved it as a snack. The best fat pieces were salted and saved to fry for fatback.

Horns To Blow

My daddy was in full charge when it was time to dehorn a bull to keep it from throwing its head and goring another animal or a person. It was one of the most gruesome experiences on a farm. Dad and one of my grandfathers and maybe some of the sawmill crew held the bull's head and then took huge clippers and clipped the horns off. Those clippers were terrible-looking things. They did this in cool weather, always before spring. That way they didn't take a chance of having flies all over the wound and the possibility of an infection setting in.

Those horns were valuable possessions and date all the way back to biblical days. Some were used as powder horns—the way for a hunter or soldier to keep his gunpowder dry. Some of ours were used as signaling horns, like the ones probably used at the Battle of Jericho. It took skill to learn to blow a signal, but I wanted to do that from the first time I saw my father pick one up and signal my grandfather when he was in the field. Our dogs learned that sound. Whenever one of us blew it, they thought it was suppertime. They'd stop whatever they were doing. If they were in the woods and heard the sound, they stopped chasing an animal and came on home looking to eat. Years later, I became the National Fox Horn Blowing Champion at Spivey's Corner.

Sewin' Sacks

Mama was a good seamstress. She made a lot of our clothes out of feed sacks. She'd tell Papa to get the same color or pattern when he went and bought feed for the animals. She made all of our shirts and pants and everything 'til we got up in size. In the meantime, all the clothes were passed among the ten young'uns 'til they were too worn out to wear. Then she'd take and use the fabric in other ways, even if it was for a washrag.

She might use small scraps and even worn-out overalls in quilts. I like to tell about how Mama never wasted anything. She had a large, handmade wood quilt frame that rose up to the ceiling by a rope and then tied to ceiling hooks. Mama would start a quilt during the daytime while most of the young'uns were at school. Then she rolled the frame up to the ceiling to get it out of the way at night, so we could walk through the room. The next mornin' she'd work on it while we were at school. Most of the time she had the top, middle, and back put together and ready to be quilted in two days. On the third day, she'd put string threads through all the layers all over the quilt.

When we got home from school, Mama had the young'uns gathered around the quilt frame helping to tie the string into knots, which is called tacking. She didn't take the time to do the quilt stitching all over. Mama could make a quilt in three days. They weren't fancy, but they kept us warm.

Sometimes, Mama got together with the other ladies who lived nearby to make a quilt. They could make it in one day. These were usually made for a new family that moved into the community or for someone who was seeing it hard.

Music Lessons

I was lucky to have two sets of good grandparents. They took time and taught us things, even though they had lots of grandchildren. I always liked visiting them. I was fascinated when my grandfather Jethro played his harmonica. He kept it lyin' on the fireboard. About every time a kid came around he'd play it. Sometimes we had to ask him. If he wasn't busy working at something, he'd get it down and play it. He loved to play it.

I was happy when he'd let me blow on it. He saw I was serious about learning, so he made an effort to teach me. He said to cover up the notes I didn't want to hear with my tongue. Then, I was to blow out of each side of my tongue.

My brother brought a jaw harp home and was sitting around playing with it. He showed me how. As soon as I could, I got one by trading something with a friend who didn't know how to play the harp. We sat around doing a lot of twanging, pretending we were making music.

Papa knew I liked the harmonica and he bought me an instrument like a Dobro when I was twelve. I had it a long time and fooled around trying to teach myself to play it. I learned to play a few simple tunes. Over the years it got busted up from so many young'uns fooling with it.

I should have known then how much music meant to my life, but I guess I took it for granted. My great-granddaddy bought an organ for the Lutheran church, but the Baptists were strict and didn't believe in instruments until sometime in the 1940s. Our Baptist music was a cappella singing. I also recall seeing my grandparents and great-aunt singing in front of the open fireplace on Saturday nights. They sang in three-part harmony. Sometimes Granddaddy pulled out his harmonica.

We all sang at church and sometimes at night after supper, and before bed, we'd have a time like a family time and we'd sing hymns with Mama. We'd almost always sing "How Tedious and Tasteless." Some called it "Without God." The words went like this:

> *How tedious and tasteless the hour*
> *When Jesus no longer I see*
> *Sweet prospect, sweet birds, sweet flowers,*
> *Have all lost their sweetness for me.*

The other favorite was "The Ninety and Nine."

> *There were ninety and nine safely laid*
> *In the shelter of the fold.*
> *But one was out on the hills away,*
> *Far off from the gates of gold.*
> *Away on the mountain wild and bare,*
> *Away from the shepherd's tender care.*
> *Away from the shepherd's tender care.*

Church, music, talking and visiting were part of the fun that was to be had when we were young'uns. We got along with each other pretty well and spent time running around. When it snowed in the winter, we liked getting out and fixing a makeshift sled that'd take us down the hill.

Birthdays were little noticed. But we did know we were a year older on that day. Most times an older sister would bake the birthday person a cake. So many of us had birthdays in June, there wasn't always a cake for each person. No matter—any cakes set on the table were gone in a little bit.

SAWMILL MEN

My father spent his life working in sawmills. He grew up learning the trade and working the mill with his uncle, my grandmother's brother, John Ford. John set up a mill and then hired my father and his three brothers to work with him as each became old enough. My great uncle owned a steam engine. The Bolick boys learned to grade lumber, saw and cruise a boundary of timber.

My father's brother Frank was the oldest. He started out on his own and then hired his brothers. He became a pretty big operator and was well known in our area. I still run into people who worked for him.

Papa's brother John looked after the mill. He was a sawyer, meaning he did the sawin' or oversaw anybody else that was sawin'. The other brother, George, looked after trucking and hauling lumber. My father was the foreman of the horses, men and timber cutting. Back then, they cut the trees with a crosscut saw with one man on each end of the saw. They cut it up into log lengths of eight, ten, twelve, fourteen or sixteen length in the woods. A single horse snaked each log out of woods to the main logging trail. Next, a team of horses would back up to two head logs, then nail grabs were used to tack two logs behind and then two more behind that if the horses were able to pull 'em. In those days, it was a large, efficient operation.

Uncle Frank got down in the eastern part of North Carolina bidding on large stands of timber. He thought it was good timber and that the market was right for him to branch out. He saw that as an opportunity to make money and took a crew of men from the mountains along with all the necessary equipment to do the job. He got there cutting timber and didn't realize that things near the coast would be different. He took men who had never been out of the mountains. That probably presented a few problems. Also, he didn't count on operating in swampy areas. He

Sawmilling was our life for four generations. "I have it in my blood," Glenn says. He has sawmilled all his life and has no plans to stop. Glenn is passing the work and the tradition on to his son. *Photograph by Jim Dollar.*

didn't know how to get the timber out of the soft ground. It must have been frustrating to see that there was a market, but not be able to get the timber out. He moved back to the mountains and started all over again.

In the meantime, Papa stayed behind. That's when he started his own crew. Then, we didn't see much of him except on weekends and when we were old enough to go out into the woods and help. My first big job came when I was ten years old. Papa set up a camp in Burke County in the south mountains. I moved around with them all summer. I'd carry water in galvanized buckets from the stream to the camp kitchen where my sister, Treva, was working as the cook for the crew. She was my oldest sister and was married. Her husband worked on the crew with Papa.

We were out in the middle of the forest all day and all night, Monday through Friday. Everyone left for the weekend to be with their families. The crew put together wooden shelters for a bunkhouse. It was a makeshift kind of building and very crude. Yet all they needed was a place to sleep at night and get out of the weather.

Papa was only at home on weekends and at the times when he had a boundary of timber to cut that was close to our house so he could come home at night. He might be home some in the winter when the snow would fall too deep or an ice storm would come in.

It didn't help Dad's business that he was constantly signing up crews. A lot of his trained men took regular jobs in the furniture factories in Lenoir. They could get regular pay and be home with their families at night. If the weather was too bad for working, the men didn't get paid.

GOING MODERN

We lived in a wood house with no conveniences. We used six or eight kerosene lamps after dark. I was too young to light the lamps, but I had to help clean the chimneys once a week. The trick to having less to clean was keeping the wicks trimmed so the glass wouldn't blacken so bad. We had a battery radio we could listen to. One of our neighbors had a radio that'd run on his car battery. Then he'd recharge his car battery with the car generator attached to a water wheel.

Papa and the grown men liked to hunt coon at night. They used lanterns to carry into the woods to help light their way. Papa had a three-cell flashlight he carried with them. He'd use it to shine up in the tree to locate the coon.

When the days got short, Mama let us stay up a little while after dark. We played games like thimble rise. The young'uns sat around in a circle. The person who was "it" had a thimble in his or her hand. He went around and pretended to put the thimble in each person's hand, but only put it in one person's. Everyone took turns guessing who was holding the thimble. The young'un who guessed right got to be "it" and pass the thimble.

Electricity didn't come until 1947. My grandparents lost their general store and all of the money they had in the bank during the Depression. They survived by farming. When the power line cut through their farm, they never hooked on to the electricity. They didn't feel they could afford it.

We were all so excited to see the electric lights and to know we wouldn't have to use kerosene lamps. We soon realized it didn't really help us any; we still had the same chores to do. It did help Mama to have a refrigerator and I guess we made fewer trips to the can house. The biggest bonus of the electricity was having a radio that didn't depend on batteries. We had the best time sitting around in the evening and especially on Saturday night listening to the different programs. We all loved hearing the Carter family. They were among the first groups I ever heard. Hearing that sound coming from the radio made a huge impression on me when I was only eleven or twelve.

We always had a vehicle. The first one I remember was a 1939 Plymouth pickup truck. That made us a little more modern than some. But Papa needed a truck for his sawmilling business. Sometimes he had both a pickup and a big lumber truck. Then he might sell his pickup and only have the lumber truck. No matter, he never had anything that would hold ten kids. We grew up standing in the back of trucks.

None of us got to town more than once a year until we were old enough to get ourselves there. Mama and Papa would take a few young'uns at a time and buy us a pair of new shoes. We'd get real excited about the trip and just as tickled to get the new shoes. Papa was the one to go to Lenoir nearly every Saturday. That's when he'd pay off some of his crew. Sometimes he took Mama and she'd do a little shopping for things we needed.

Leavin' Home

My brother Boyd and his close friend Kenneth Hollars and I left home when we were about eighteen. That's when it was thought we were old enough to be on our own. It just seemed like it was time to do something on my own. Papa was startin' to ease up on sawmilling. When we got a little settled, we started sending a little money home. Mama was always good with money. She had been Papa's bookkeeper and did his income taxes and all.

My sister Reba married Alfred Ford. He traveled with Clement Brothers of Hickory and was contracted for work with Coleman Contracting, a rock-crushing business. He was in charge of an operation in Joanna, South Carolina. He needed workers and on a trip home he asked us to come and work with him. He bought a trailer so my sister could go too.

It was the first time I'd ever been out of the mountains and everything was new. It was interesting to be in flat country seeing how people farmed without the high mountain plowing. Also the work was different from anything I'd ever experienced. When my brother and I saw all that big road equipment for the first time, we couldn't wait to learn how to run it.

We crushed stone for the state highway system and stockpiled it for use in building roads. I ran the bulldozer, drove a truck, and got pretty good pay. They started me at $1.25 an hour in 1958. After a few weeks I was getting the top pay of $1.50 an hour and could do any job including the power shovel and loading trucks with a track loader. I was away from home, not married and had all that money.

My first check of $63.00 for one week's work was the most money I had ever made. I had worked in the furniture factory in Lenoir and didn't make over $28.00 to $30.00 for a week. The plant operated twenty-four hours a day. Most of the time I was in Johanna, I worked two shifts and got twice the pay.

Next, I took the job of feeding the jaw crusher. Then I moved on to running the crushing plant. There was a switchboard with a sequence of buttons that got the belts and motors running. I learned not to shut the crusher off first or we'd have a lot of hand labor to remove the gravel before it could be restarted.

Boyd, Kenneth and I loved the work. Runnin' those big machines was fun. It made us feel like we had power at our fingertips. I've always liked to work outside, so it was easy for me to learn to operate all the equipment and learn to drive those big trucks. I also learned to be careful. Once I forgot to release the tailgate lever on a dump truck loaded with gravel. When the bed went back without the tailgate open, it put the cab about twelve feet in the air. I'd seen one of my father's crewmen do that while dumping slab wood. But, there I was up in the air in that same predicament.

All the weight was in the back and I couldn't open the tailgate. I had to get the bed back down. I eased the truck in reverse with the back wheels pulling. If the front end went down too quickly, the cab would have hit the ground and taken me forward into the windshield. It mighta killed me.

We stayed there for nine months living in a boarding house. We ate out at the Hawkins Café every night. Even though we had to pay for all of our living expenses, we still sent money home. By then, my father's health was not good and he wasn't able to work so much. The little we sent home helped a lot.

After a few months, my brother and I decided we were making enough money to buy a car. We bought a secondhand 1958 Fairlane Ford 500. It was black and gold. We had a ball driving around seeing what we could see. We didn't have to worry about catching a ride and it was better than walking.

After that, we were sent to Orange County, North Carolina, on the Eno River. We decided for what we spent in a boarding house we could have more room if we bought a trailer. The company had surveyed a quarry location so we could blast rock for building Interstate 85. We got there before the rest of the crew and removed eight or ten feet of dirt over approximately two acres so the quarry could get started.

We were hoping the move would get us a little raise in pay, but Superior Stone bought out Bob Coleman and the company was so tight we couldn't get a raise. They told us the only reason we were making $1.50 an hour was because we were already receiving that pay when they bought the company.

We moved our trailer to Hillsborough and stayed in a trailer park. About then, my brother got drafted into the army and I was left with Kenneth as my roommate. I gave my brother some money and took up the car payments and the trailer payment. I had time on my hands after work and that's when I bought a guitar and banjo.

I enjoyed knowing William Hicks, who lived nearby. Function Station railroad track ran through his property. Mrs. Hicks said her grandfather had the job of lighting signal lanterns for the railroad way back in the 1800s.

The Hicks had a friend that came by, and we'd sit and play instruments in our spare time. I worked to accompany myself singing the old songs I remembered and traded a few tunes with my friends. That got me into regularly playing guitar and trying to remember old songs. Every chance I got I learned something new. Mama copied down songs and sent them to me in the mail. I'd get one on my mind and would write her and let her know I wanted to learn it. Sometimes I could remember the tune but not the words.

That was the time I realized how much music had come my way. All the old hymns from church and the old songs I heard at corn shuckin's came back to me. I started singing and recalling the words. I practiced every chance I got. A few of us playing together got to sound pretty good. At least I thought so.

Two years went by and Kenneth and I were sent to Asheboro to start stripping land to open a new quarry to produce rock for Highway 220. The first night we were there, we went to eat at Tommy's Drive-In Grill. We rolled down our window and talked to the two girls seated in their car beside ours.

Lula Owens and I met a few more times at Tommy's and we enjoyed talking to each other. She worked third shift at the mill, so many of our dates involved going to the drive-in and sitting around talking before she had to go to work. When I asked her to go home to meet my mother, her mother wouldn't let her spend the night and required we have a chaperone. I took her younger brother and younger sister with us. They were the same age as my two younger brothers. We got up early for the long drive and then spent the time we had seeing the sights in Blowing Rock and on Grandfather Mountain.

On the way home, we stopped at a grill in Lexington to have something to eat. That was probably the happiest day of my life. I had twenty-five dollars in my pocket. The four of us had a good time eating hamburgers, fries and shakes. Lula and her brother and sister had never seen the mountains. The conversation was all about the things they'd seen. I felt like a hero. It was a perfect day.

Lula Owens married Glenn Bolick. After eleven years of living in Seagrove, North Carolina, they took their pottery talents to Bolick Road in the Bailey's Camp community near Blowing Rock where they have a pottery shop and an amphitheater for free summer Sunday afternoon concerts. *Photograph by B. Salsi.*

I was twenty-two and ready to settle down. I asked Lula to marry me and got permission from her mother and father. We spent ten years in Seagrove. Her family taught me how to make pottery. I spent time with my two children and learned about business. We made trips to see my mother every chance we got. With every trip, I got more and more homesick. I missed the open land, the landscape, the beauty of the clouds hanging over the mountain and the snow in the winter. When I found out my great-grandfather and grandfather's land was to be sold, I started talking Lula into moving and I started talking to the owner figuring out how I could get the property back in our family.

MOUNTAIN HOME

When I bought my great-grandfather's farm in 1973, it meant I moved my family back to the land where I was raised and to the house that was part of my life from the day I was born. My mama's house and land was across the narrow dirt road and two of my brothers lived down the road. We were back living on the family land again.

I moved my guitar and banjo, too. I'd spent years strumming and picking and sitting around singing for my own entertainment. Lula played the guitar and we enjoyed relaxing and singing together.

It got on my mind to join a band. I loved to sing and knew it. Bob Harmon was the lead man with a band called the Blue Ridge Descendents. I heard them playing around our area for a lot of events. They didn't have singing. Bob had made an album or two—all instrumental.

I'd run into Bob Harmon from time to time, and finally I asked him if I could join the group as a singer. I'm sure I asked four or five times. I knew they didn't have a singer and there was room for me to join. He'd say, "We don't have any singin' in our group." I just went on sitting around in my front room playing my guitar and practicing singing at church and around anyone who'd listen.

In 1974, I decided to go over to Lenoir to a fiddlers' convention. I took my guitar and harmonica and went by myself to see what everyone else was playing, thinking I could meet some people and learn a few new tunes. There were all kinds of different groups sitting round practicin' before they went on stage to compete. There was an old-timey string group in a corner. They caught my ear because they were playing the kind of music I like.

I got closer and they knew I was listening to them play. One of 'em said, "Come on over and play a little with us." I sat with them for a while and jammed. We got along fine. It was Arlie Watson, his wife, Ora, Arnold Watson (Doc Watson's brother) and Paul Greer. Paul made a comment as to how he liked my singing, and how I might want to join 'em sometime. That built me up. Later they went on stage and played.

Then, later in 1974, on the first Sunday in June, the Blue Ridge Descendents played for our Bolick family reunion. It's held each year to honor Great-grandfather Marcus's birthday. They started playing and I got up and sang along to a few of their tunes. I couldn't help myself; I just love to sing.

Bob Harmon loved it so much he asked me to come along and sing for some of their gigs. Back then, playing in a band didn't have anything to do with money. People got together and played because they loved music. I was tickled to be asked to sing in front of audiences. A few times we might get travel money and a meal. In the summer, we played often for the tourists at Price Park on the Blue Ridge Parkway.

Glenn recycles old barn wood in reconstructing buildings and fences on his property. It gives that old-timey, authentic appearance and helps keep in the horses and cows. *Photograph by Jim Dollar.*

Glenn Bolick

Music and storytelling are Glenn's favorite pastimes. He travels to schools, libraries, museums and fiddle competitions to entertain. He is shown above with Ora Watson at an appearance at the Cove Creek Senior Citizens' Center. He and Ora played in various bands over the past thirty years. *Photograph by B.Salsi.*

Glenn built the fretless groundhog banjo he plays during musical performances. He enjoys carrying out old mountain traditions and crafts. "Making the banjo is harder than you think. I got instrument maker Charlie Glenn at Sugar Grove to help me finish it. I also get a lot of help with my instruments from Alfred Michels in Creston," Glenn said. *Photograph by B. Salsi*

Glenn saved many old outbuildings from destruction and reconstructed them on his land. They are the setting for the Heritage Day his family sponsors the Saturday before July 4th each year. *Photograph by B. Salsi.*

There were five or six in the group, depending on who could show up. Rand Shook was the oldest member. He was a retired sawmiller and a super banjo player. I liked hearing him tell sawmill stories. He knew how to hammer saws and gum saws to make 'em run right. That was a skill not many people had. He was in demand to play banjo a lot of places. He loved to go to "Singing on the Mountain" at Grandfather Mountain. One year he got invited to play with a Scottish group. Some of us happened to go by his house when he was loading up. We got a good laugh seeing him standing there with a kilt on. We knew then that he'd do most anything to get to entertain. A little while after Rand died, Bob Harmon disbanded the group.

During the time I was playing with Bob's group, I was invited to play with Ora, Arlie, Paul and Arnold. They called their group the Blue Ridge Ramblers. For a while, I played with both groups. Back then, there weren't a lot of gigs that paid money and most of us appreciated getting a little pay, even if it meant passing the hat. The Ramblers played right much and sometime Doc Watson came and sat in with us. We got a regular slot at Sims Country Barbeque in Dudley Shoals, which is between Hickory and Wilkesboro. They had good barbeque, live music and square dancing.

I still have a lot of fun playing old-timey music and sharing it with audiences. I lead the singing at church and we stick to singing the ole gospel tunes. I sit in with different bands. Some play only old mountain tunes and a few mix in some blue grass. Some Saturdays in the summer, I sit in the plaza in Blowing Rock in front of our Bolick's pottery shop and pick and sing. Many tourists come over and enjoy the local flavor.

Editor's note:
Glenn Bolick was born to an Appalachian Mountain heritage he has worked for thirty years to save. Unlike many children who grew up under hard physical labor and left the mountains in their adult years, Glenn worked at various jobs off the mountain only to return home to the family land. He feels a kindred spirit to past generations and to his family. As the keeper of mountain traditions, he is passing his love of music, storytelling and farming on to his children and their children.

Glenn performed at the World's Fair in Knoxville and appeared on the *Pat Sajak Show*. He's the winner of the Spivey's Corner National Hollerin' Contest and the Spivey's Corner Fox Horn Blowin' Contest. Glenn and his wife, Lula, were honored by the North Carolina Folklore Society with the Brown-Hudson Folklore Award. Their pottery, representing four generations of Owens and Bolick pottery, is on display in the North Carolina History Museum in Raleigh.

The Bolick family sponsors Heritage Day the last Sunday in June and Kiln Opening Days in Novemeber at their pottery shop on Bolick Road off Highway 321 near Blowing Rock, North Carolina. Glenn is the author of a book, *If This Ain't True, Grits Ain't Groceries*.

Don Dotson worked in the WPA during the Great Depression, when the roads through the Appalachian Mountains were widened from narrow paths and trails to roads that could accommodate trucks and cars. Robert's father is on the front row (left), sitting in a wheelbarrow. *Photograph courtesy of the Dotson collection.*

ROBERT DOTSON

CHAMPION FLATFOOTER, DANCE CALLER AND 'BACCER FARMER

I helped my family by farmin', timberin', sawmillin', growin' 'baccer and raisin' horses and cows. I did that all my life. But it's dancin' I like to talk about. I've danced and loved music all my life. It's mountain dancin'—a lot that's gone out of style. It's ole-timey—nothin' fancy. But there's skill to it, for it to be good.

EARLY DAYS

My family on my grandmother's side goes back to the history of Sugar Grove community in the 1800s. The Wards in my family were among the first people to come to the mountains when it was Indian Territory. My grandpa was Albert Dotson. Everyone called him Ab. He came to this area from West Virginia from the coal mines. I tell people he was "loafin' around and lookin' for a job. But he was tryin' to get away from the mines." He found farm work in Sugar Grove and married Sis Ward. That's how the Dotson name got to the area in the late 1800s.

Granddaddy farmed and all—everybody had to farm or they'd had nothin' to eat. But Ab Dotson was also known for layin' out dead people. When he'd get the word somebody had passed away, he walked or rode his horse the three or four miles over to work on the men to have 'em presentable to be buried. He dressed the men and shaved 'em. He took a woman with him to dress the ladies. There was no way of preservin' the bodies. He went three or four miles right away when called. The body 'ud have to be ready for a burial the next day.

Granddaddy also pulled teeth. He was the only dentist for miles around. I don't know that he ever got any pay for his burial services or his dentistry. He mighta sometimes got a chicken or some vegetables. He mostly did it because he had the skill and wanted to help his neighbors.

Granddaddy also farmed his land and raised livestock. He did pretty good for the times. Back then if you had a horse and buggy people looked up to ya. If you had two horses, it was thought you were pretty well off. He was known for workin' hard. He got work on with the WPA (Works Progress Administration) during the Great Depression. In 1934 he made a little money goin' out workin' to get better roads so people could get in and out of the mountains. And, he got a good dinner meal out of it too.

My dad, Don Dotson, was Ab's son. He married my mama, Bina Jane Hicks, and they farmed and raised eight young'uns. I was the oldest. Daddy was also a moonshiner, but not in any big way. He made enough to drink himself and have some for others to drink durin' social gatherin's like beanstringin's, corn shuckin's and wood gettin's.

Robert Dotson teaches students of all ages about mountain dancing. He works hard to keep mountain traditions alive and to preserve the art of old-style dancing. *Photograph by B. Salsi.*

Left: Bina Jean Hicks Dotson was Robert's mother. She was the best flatfoot dancer in Watauga County. *Photograph courtesy of the Dotson Collection.*

Right: Don Dotson, Robert's dad, farmed, played music and danced. Music was part of the family's life. *Photograph courtesy of the Dotson Collection.*

Church meetin's and gatherin's with neighbors to work were the times the young'uns looked forward to. We'd all visit around helpin' each other to get the big work done. Afterward there'd be food, music, dancin' and the men 'ud get a drink of 'shine. Those are the times that were the most fun for me.

Mama taught me to dance and I had fun from the first time I tried. It was in my blood. I never stopped from the time I was eight or ten.

I got to go to the old school that wasn't too far from our house. I remember walkin' and takin' corn bread and milk in my little tin. Sometimes I put the cornbread in the milk that was in a pint can. That was what I had for dinner most days. But meals were simple then. There was mostly water and milk if I was lucky.

My schoolin' stopped in 1935 when Dad fell off the back of a truck. He went to Boone to see a performance by Uncle Dave Macon and caught a ride home. The vehicle hit a bump or something when it got to Vilas. Dad hit his head and it killed him. It left Mama figurin' out how to raise the eight young'uns by herself. I quit school, got out and worked like a man to help her. I was almost thirteen years old. From then on, I saw nothin' but work ahead of me.

Back then there was a lot of superstitions goin' round. Most had to do with signs. They were written in the *Blum's Almanac*. If somebody didn't own a *Blum's*, they'd likely go to their neighbors and borrow one. People back then didn't do anything unless the almanac said to. They wouldn't kill hogs or plant gardens. They wouldn't make kraut or can their harvest if the signs weren't right.

I've been married to my wife, Myrtle, for nearly sixty years. We've gotten over all that stuff about superstitions and signs. It's better we now have ways to know more about the weather than our parents did. I did a lot of 'baccer farmin' to have a cash crop. After years of livin' on the same land and farmin' the same way, I got to the place I had confidence in my experience and knowledge of how to do things.

I've always planted a big garden for us to have plenty to eat to see us through all the seasons of the year. I planted a lot of cabbages, corn, tomatoes, Irish potatoes, beans, squash, onions and pumpkins. Myrtle and my daughters keep our can house full. I also like huntin' and provided squirrel, rabbit and deer for cannin'—the same way as my daddy and granddaddy did.

Myrtle has chopped a lot of cabbage to make kraut. This is how she does it.

Hack up the cabbage pretty fine and put it in clean half-gallon glass jars. Add one tablespoon of salt per jar. Put the top on, but not tight. Then let the cabbage work. The water'll work out of it and more water has to be added to keep the cabbage covered or it will lose its color. When it quits workin' the water out, the tops can be screwed on tight. Then, put it on a shelf in the can house and let it sit.

BORN TO DANCE

I was born to dance. My father and mother played guitar and banjo the ole-timey way. From the time I was a young'un, they enjoyed gettin' together with people around to entertain. There was a time they went to a dance at somebody's house every Saturday night. They called one or two square dances, but it was mostly flatfootin'. Both my parents were good dancers, but my mother could dance the best. She loved it. In her day, she was considered the finest flatfoot dancer in Watauga County. It was something when I got to go with 'em to a dance. I never tried to play music. I just wanted to dance.

Robert spent years growing tobacco. Burley tobacco is grown in the mountains and cured in barns like the one shown above. *Photograph by B. Salsi.*

In the 1920s, the churches frowned on dancin'—'specially the Baptist. We had to kinda slip around to dance. That's why much of our fun was with our family and neighbors. Back then, we weren't out in public with it. That didn't come along until fiddle festivals and music festivals got big.

We all knew there was far worse things than dancin'. Drinkin' too much, gossipin' and lyin' is much worse than dancin'. It gave us some fun and gave fun to others. My parents figured it couldn't be too bad if it brought a little happiness. So, we kept on doin' it.

That's why I'm a flatfooter. I wanted to be as good a dancer as my mother. What helps me is not patternizing no one. I stick to the steps I learned from Mama and from the ones I set my way. But when it comes to styles, I can do it all—buck dancin', flatfootin', square dancin' and the two step.

Most people think of mountain dancin' as buck dancin' and cloggin'. But flatfootin' shows skill. Buck dancin' has kickin' and some stompin'. Although I can do it, it's a little rough and looks a little rowdy. Cloggin's mostly for young'uns. They have to have taps on their shoes and it makes one big racket. Sometimes a bunch of 'em dancin' together get so loud the band can't play.

Now, I ain't sayin' there's anything bad about it. Some like it. But I think real dancin' is more about skill. Flatfootin' is the best. There has to be a good lead at any kind of a dance to make it look good. In square dancin' there has to be cooperation from all the dancers. They have to follow directions from the caller. In flatfootin' the dancer has to have good balance and be sure of his steps. If a person's in a flatfootin' competition and starts stompin' around, they'll lose. If I don't hold my feet down I won't win. It all comes from my head and heart and then goes to my feet. That's when I have to do something about it. In the ole times, if judges could hear too much noise from a dancer's feet, they'd pull 'em off the floor and tell 'em, "You're stompin', not dancin'."

It's been a while back, but I won the state championship. I've danced for every event I can think of except funerals. I've performed for weddings, anniversaries and festivals. I've even danced in church.

Myrtle and I led the dancin' in Lizzybethton [Elizabethtown], Tennessee, at Slagle's Pasture for twenty-two years. Slagle's was like an old barn. They built a stage up in the front for the band. When we went to a dance, we danced. We didn't sit around on the bench. We'd dance so long at times there wouldn't be a dry hair on our heads. We'd turn the heat on in the car to dry off on our ride home.

Robert squared danced with his wife, Myrtle, and with Verona Miller (pictured above). Verona's husband called the dances. *Photograph courtesy of the Dotson collection.*

We met Verona Miller and her husband over at Slagle's startin' back in the late '70s. I square danced with her some for twelve years or so. Her husband was callin' the dances. When he couldn't come, I'd call the dance. When Slagle's was goin' strong, hundreds of dancers hit the floor on the first beat. They'd do three or four square dances, but the rest of the time the floor was packed with flatfooters.

When my grandchildren got up a little in size, I've taken off with 'em in my camper to go to festivals. We might stay a week. Myrtle 'ud fall in there with us if she could. If she had cannin' or something and couldn't go, I might take the young'uns and go on without her. If I was on stage competin', people at the festivals 'ud help me take care of 'em.

I still like fiddlin' and dancin' festivals and look forward to goin' every chance I get. I can dance all night. I've danced forty-five minutes straight without restin' and not gotten tired. If you like doin' something, you'd better get out and do it. That's why I'm still dancin', and I'm nigh on to eighty-four years old.

When I hear music, it gets my rhythm goin'. Myrtle tells people that if I hear a song I like on the radio while I'm drivin' I go crazy and have to pull over. She's about right. I want to dance every time I hear the right tune. I remember going down the road one evening with Earl Phillips. We heard a tune we liked on the radio and I pulled over. We got out and danced in front of the headlights. I really like "Down Yonder" and "Katie Hill." They might be my two favorites to dance to. Those are tunes that make a peg-legged man want to pat his foot. But if I'm a mind to tap my foot and do a little dancin', I can make up a tune in my head and dance to it without instruments.

I like teachin' flatfoot dancin' and I get called to go all over North Carolina, Kentucky, Virginia and Tennessee to show students how it's done. Style is part of the tradition. Once students get the step and practice it, they can concentrate more on the music and enjoy themselves.

I don't get into music that's played too fast. I can't get all my steps in and it takes away my energy. When I teach dancin' at some of the colleges, I tell 'em to take a break when they get tired. If they stay out on the dance floor, they'll start messin' up their steps.

I tell 'em not to dance on concrete. It's too hard on the feet and legs. Flatfootin' has to be on a wood floor that has a little give to it. The steps look better. If I dance on concrete, people are likely to look at me and say, "He's done messed up."

Flatfootin' requires more skill in keepin' the feet close to the floor. It looks smoother. When people jump out and start stompin' around and kickin' up their feet, it's not dancin'. People used to say a good flatfooter could dance on a lookin' glass and not break it.

The cabin was filled with music and dancing on weekends. Robert built it and "they came" from as far as New York City. *Photograph by B. Salsi.*

The arms are important to help the rhythm. When I enter a contest, I think to hold my feet down and have my arms doin' the right motion. Winners of these competitions use their entire body. It's not enough to mark rhythm with the feet. The entire body has to look good.

I liked ole-timey string-band music. All I need's a fiddle, guitar and banjo playin' for me. It's the real mountain music. Bluegrass came along and I still think of it as modern. It's good to listen to, but I can't dance to it. It's too fast and has too much a sound like it ought to be heard on radio, not played at a dance. If I'm leadin' a dance and the band plays bluegrass, I sit down and listen.

Most of all, I enjoy hearin' the clappin' for my dancin'. It makes me think I'm doin' okay. If I didn't get a hand, I'd think something was wrong with my feet. I'd have to take a break and get it goin' right.

I liked the old music and the old dancin' so much I built a cabin across the road from my house just for fun. The dance floor was a 24 feet wide by 32 feet long open space. I fixed the wood floor in that place—right. During the early '70s we opened it up and held parties there for six or seven years. People came from all over the mountains to have a good time. The Corklickers out of Boone was one of the regular bands—when those guys were real young.

The place was always full. Cars 'ud pull in and fill up the pasture below the cabin. Everybody liked to come to get away from their worries and have a good time. I built an apartment downstairs so musicians could stay overnight if they needed to.

Ribbons and trophies fill a room in the Dotson home. Robert won the North Carolina state championship among many fiddler festival dance competitions. *Photograph by B. Salsi.*

Robert Dotson dances for fun, trophies, ribbons—and most of all, for joy. He was born to dance. *Photograph by B. Salsi.*

I was lucky to grow up around a lot of great old-timey musicians. I knew Stanley Hicks real well. He was a good musician and handmade a lot of delcimores [dulcimers] and groundhog banjos. Everybody knew him. He was funny and a good entertainer. He played a lot of times I was dancin'.

Ora Watson's in her nineties now, but still plays the fiddle. She spent many a Saturday night playin' fiddle for the dancers in my cabin. She could hang in with the best of 'em and knew hundreds of old tunes. She was something to see when she'd get up and dance and play the fiddle at the same time. Now, when she did that, the crowd 'ud go wild.

Tommy Jarrell came and played too. He was a great old-time fiddler from Mount

Airy. He came once and played all night. The next morning I told him he had to excuse me while I went out and fed my cattle. They have a Tommy Jarrell Festival to honor him, and I go over to dance for that each year.

One day, somebody called from New York City and asked if they could come to perform at the cabin. I said, "Sure you can." When I got off the phone and was walkin' up to the house I was thinkin' now who would want to come all that way to dance way back here in the mountains. They pulled up with a big fancy bus like Ralph Stanley's. It was the Fiddle Puppet Cloggers with six or eight dancers. I started dancin' with 'em. They took me all the way to New York City once to perform with 'em. I've known Rodney Sutton ever since. He's now in Asheville, and I still see him sometime.

Myrtle and I kept on dancin' together till Myrtle's health kept her off the dance floor. But that was not before we won the North Carolina Folk Heritage Award in 1994. The people in the North Carolina History Museum in Raleigh kept our dancin' shoes to put on display in an exhibit.

I buy all my dancin' shoes in Mountain City, Tennessee. I have to have special leather-soled ones. It was hard for me to leave that nice pair in Raleigh; they were broken in good. That's not easy since dancin' shoes can't be worn on the street. I'd like to go back one day to see 'em on display in a glass case.

I've always got a lot out of dancin'. I've made a lot of friends and had a lot of good times. When I hear the music start, it lifts me and makes me want to get out and dance. It's good to get this far in life and still be lookin' forward to the next dance.

Editor's note:
Robert Dotson is an amazing octogenarian. And, he can't stop dancing. He appears at Merle Fest in Wilkesboro, North Carolina, each year. He's featured at the Tommy Jarrell Festival in Mount Airy, North Carolina, and at many other festivals in North Carolina, Tennessee, Virginia and West Virginia. Robert can be found at Warren Wilson College each year teaching and demonstrating many versions of ole-timey dancin'. He enjoys sharing his knowledge and has taught hundreds of students from New York City to North Carolina.

Amy Michels says Robert might not dance on concrete, but he sure can dance on plywood when a temporary stage is required. She said, "Throw a little cornmeal on that plywood and it keeps the ole-timey flavor goin'. If it's self-risin' cornmeal, it makes Robert's feet rise a little."

ORA WATSON

CHAMPION FIDDLER, DANCER
AND ENTERTAINER

I was born in June of 1911 and grew up Ora Isaacs on Isaacs Branch in the Bethel area on the lower end of Old Beech Mountain. My parents moved from the Beaver Dam community when Daddy bought a forty-six-acre farm.

My family played old-timey music. Most of the Isaacs cousins were known for playing music. Mother sang in church and Daddy played a homemade banjo. He was a real good musician and a good buck dancer.

Daddy drove us in a horse-drawn buggy every Sunday to the Cove Creek Baptist Church. We knew they didn't like any kind of dancin' or carryin' on. But music was our entertainment and we were glad we could do it. It got us a little notice in our community.

My sisters and I picked up music from our parents and grandparents. By the time I was ten or eleven we had our own string band and played all around as the Isaacs Sisters. In the early 1920s we went to Bristol, Tennessee, and played on the radio. My mother didn't care for any hillbilly music; to her, it was from the devil. She taught me to play hymns and moral kinda music on the fiddle.

I learned to play a lot of different tunes from different people. In my life I knew more than one hundred. Some of them are so old they've almost been forgotten. None of 'em were ever written down. They passed down within families.

My daddy taught me "The Old TB." It went like this:

This is the story of two and they loved each other more than anyone knew. The girl she took the old consumption and broke the boy's heart you know.

Ora Watson started playing the fiddle when she was old enough to hold one. She married young and gave up music to raise her four children. She is shown above as a young woman around 1929. *Photograph courtesy of the Watson collection.*

Back in those old-timey days they sang songs about lost love. Words told about murder and wayward people. Some of the other songs I liked were "Wild Bill Jones" and "On the Banks of the Ohio." My daddy taught me "Careless Love" and my mother liked "Drunkard's Hell." Even though she favored hymns, she thought it had a lesson in it. It told about the bad fate of drunkards. After I married, my husband's grandmother taught me a few songs. I guess some of those went back to the middle 1800s.

Our little group played at a lot of fiddle competitions. We went all around because we won a lot. That meant we'd win a little money. I played the fiddle and my sisters played the mandolin and guitar. There was another group of sisters—the Cook Sisters—and we competed with them often. Mostly we won, but they won sometimes.

I can't remember which group it was, but one Saturday night, we were standin' backstage and one of the girls competin' against us said, "Let me see your bow for a minute."

Not thinkin' anything, I handed her my bow. With a big smile on her face, she dragged my bow through her greasy hair. Then, it was our time to go on next. That ol' hair grease kept me from playin' worth anything. We lost. I can still see that girl's big ol' grin. I knew we were good. She had to think so too, or she wouldn't have cheated to win.

I'd get in the dance competition too. I'd win the dancin' as much as for playin' my fiddle. It was good to get the prize money.

I played that fiddle as my main instrument for years and then when I was a teenager, I decided I'd rather play the guitar. I did well with that too. It came to the place I was only playin' guitar. Back then, there were no lessons, except what my daddy showed me. I tried out several styles.

One day when I was about fifteen, I was walkin' down Main Street in Boone with my guitar. I was probably goin' to sit around and play somewhere. It was usual to see musicians gathered at a store or some public place sittin' around playin' together.

I got close to where the bar was and I could see some fightin'—two men were fightin'. When I got closer, I saw my daddy was one of 'em. It looked like he was losin', so I walked over and took my guitar and busted it over the other man's head. That was the end of a good guitar, but it kept my daddy from being beat up. Anyway, I knew my mother would be real mad if she knew he was down there anywhere near a bar. Now, that doesn't mean he was goin' to the bar. He coulda been goin' to play fiddle somewhere.

Ora Watson is pictured above with her children. When they grew up, she started playing the fiddle and played with many different bands. *Photograph courtesy of the Watson collection.*

Ora is a musician's musician. She plays guitar and banjo. Most people have only seen her with a fiddle in her hand. Here she is playing banjo. *Photograph courtesy of the Michels collection.*

The law came up with the other man just lyin' there. I was scared to death I'd get taken to jail. The lawman looked at me like he was sizin' me up. I guess he saw my age and my small size. Then he said, "I guess if that was my daddy, I'd do the same thing." That was all that was ever said. I never knew what they were fightin' about. But, Daddy and I went on home and I never heard anything about it again.

I played up 'til I got married to preacher Roe Payne's son and we moved to Blowing Rock. We started farmin' and raisin' young'uns. Farm work and raisin' four young'uns didn't leave time to play music. I put my fiddle and guitar down and spent my time farmin', cookin', cleanin' and cannin'.

We lived there for about twelve years until 1942, when my husband got killed before our fourth young'un was born. I moved back home to Isaacs Branch with three young'uns and me about to have the fourth. It was with the goodness and help of my parents that I was able to raise my young'uns.

When they all left home, I got so lonesome livin' by myself, I picked up the fiddle again. The ole songs started comin' back to me and I started gettin' asked to play lots of places. I played all around for over fifty years. I sat out and played in front of the Mast Store in Valle Crucis. I played fiddlers' conventions, and played in three or four groups at the time. Mary Greene, Amy Michels and I were the Cacklin' Hens for over twenty-five years.

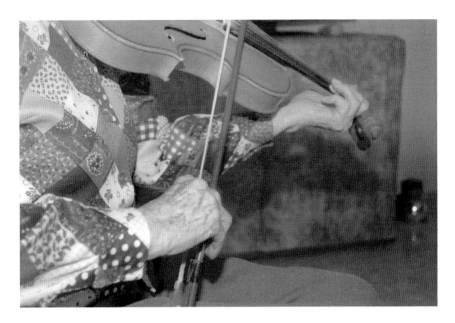

The hands of a master fiddle player. Ora is considered one of the best fiddle players ever produced in the mountains. She's played for thousands of performances, dances, festivals, education days and, at one point, sat outside of the Mast General Store playing on Saturday afternoons. *Photograph by B. Salsi.*

Jack Guy was sellin' folks toys near Beech Creek. He got me to come to his place and play fiddle on Saturday evenin's. He wanted me to help attract tourists to his store. I'd sit out front a-playin' and singin.' Arlie Watson come over with his guitar. He was a good player. We got to likin' playin' together and started playin' round lots of places. I ended up marryin', and him twenty years younger than me.

We went everywhere. We'd run into people at a club in Boone who invited us to go outside of the mountain area. We went to Florida and up and down the East Coast playin' in clubs and for dances and festivals.

Arlie liked to take a drink. We'd get aggravated with each other. One time we were on stage entertainin' and he told the audience I was wearin' a wig. That wasn't true. I had long hair hangin' down my back and him thinkin' that was funny. That got me mad. I got back at him by sayin' to the audience, "Don't you think Arlie would look better if he took his hat off?" 'Cause underneath that hat he was shiny bald with just a few hairs around the edge. People who knew him knew he kept his hat on all the time.

Ora was a regular at the Senior Citizens' Center in Boone and in Cove Creek for many years. The seniors hold a weekly jam session before lunch. Ora is shown above at the center in Boone. *Photograph by B. Salsi.*

I'm almost ninety-six and have inner-ear problems that keep me from playin' much anymore. But I sometimes pick up that ol' fiddle and go over to the senior citizens' center and jam a little.

PLAYIN' IN A BAND WITH ORA
BY AMY MICHELS

Senior citizens met at the center at Cove Creek each week to play music for fun. That's where I met Ora Watson. We ended up playin' music together for nearly thirty years.

Mary Greene and I played together with Ora as the "Cacklin' Hens." She was in her sixties and I was probably nineteen. She was a character and known by everybody. Ora is among the best fiddle players of old traditional music I've ever heard and she knows more songs than anyone. She knows songs all the way back to before she was born. She learned 'em from her parents, her grandparents and her first husband's grandmother. She doesn't mind sharin' 'em.

When the "Cacklin' Hens" played, Ora kinda took on talkin' to the audience. We'd get on stage, and Ora 'ud say, "I'm the ole settin' hen and they're the pullets."

Once we had to ask my husband, Alfred, to play music with us. Ora introduced him as "the ole rooster."

ORA WATSON, FIDDLE PLAYER
BY AMY MICHELS

Back in the late seventies, I started playin' music with Ora Watson regularly. She was in her late sixties then, so she was already old enough to get away with doin' and sayin' as she pleased. I was young and still learnin' new tunes. She was good to share what she knew. I always tried to be respectful of her age and her knowledge of music and playin' instruments.

I stopped by Ora's house one day to visit and she had a box of secondhand clothes for me. I never really care much about dressin' up too nice, but Ora likes pretty dresses and makeup and sech. She's always been a pretty woman and looked much younger than her real age. She had me try on some dresses right there at her house. One was cut for women with a full figure on top, which is exactly what I am not. She looked me over and declared I'd probably have to wear a padded bra. Then she felt of me, and decided I definitely needed to wear one.

Another time I was with her, she talked about the meanness she'd gotten into when she was a young'un. Some of the things were kinda funny and the things a young'un might do. After a while, I finally told her she was ornery. I just assumed that meant she was full of devilish fun pranks. We kinda laughed when I said that.

It wasn't long after that she called me on the phone. She said she'd looked the word "ornery" up in the dictionary and it meant a mean evil person. I told her I didn't know that, and that's not what I meant. I was hopin' she knew I didn't mean anything bad. I was teasin' her. But nothin' else was said.

Several years later, the subject came up again, only time had changed the story to my advantage. This time, she was tellin' me about how another, as she put it, "ol' woman" was being ugly to her and sayin' hateful things to her. Then she added as to how several years ago, this "ol'

Ora and Alfred Michels are shown above. When Alfred filled in with the "Cacklin' Hens," Ora introduced him as "the old rooster." *Photograph courtesy of the Michels collection.*

woman" had called her ornery, and she looked the word up and found out what it meant.

I'm sure she got her story mixed up a little, but I was smart enough to know when to keep my mouth shut that time. And, I've never thought to call anyone anything I didn't know the meaning of again. At least, I've tried.

Ora Can Put on a Show
By Glenn Bolick

Shortly after I met Ora Watson, her husband Arlie, Arnold Watson and Paul Greer at a fiddlers' convention in 1974, Arnold ran into me and asked me to join them on stage sometime. The first time I showed up with my guitar and harmonica, Arlie Watson let them know he didn't like me. He said out loud, "We don't need anybody else."

Everybody else was nice and acted like I was welcome. When we practiced, Arlie was so mad he turned his back on me. Arnold said, "Don't worry about him. He'll get over it."

Arlie had a strong lead voice. I could sing tenor as strong as he could sing, so when he found out I could harmonize with him, he stopped objecting. He started liking me. Arlie was a character, but he was a good musician. He and Ora played together. They were talented musicians and were great entertainers.

I wasn't with them very long before Arlie passed away. Then the band became me, Ora, Arnold and Paul Greer. We played at Sims Barbeque together once a week for a number of years. Then, Jim Earp joined us. That was about the time I had a lot going on with the sawmilling business and the pottery business. I was unable to play every week and dropped out of the group.

A little while after that, I got a call from people at a national dance festival at Duke University in Durham, North Carolina, asking if I'd come and play music with Ora. They wanted her to come and play her fiddle and dance, but she wasn't used to being on stage by herself. She said she'd entertain if they got me to come and sit on stage and perform with her.

Ora was used to dancing with three or four people playing behind her. She loved to dance, but was kinda shy about just gettin' right up in front of everybody. We'd play tunes awhile before we'd get Ora dancin'. We knew people loved to see her dance. Sometimes she danced while she

Glenn Bolick and Ora
have played together
for years. They're
shown above at the
Cove Creek Senior
Citizens' Center taking
a break before lunch.
Photograph by B. Salsi.

played the fiddle. She knew all kinds of flatfootin' steps. She had one she called "snake in the grass." Sometimes she'd do the Charleston. She never just hopped up and danced; she had to have a little encouragement. The audience had to clap and cheer.

I'd say, "Now, Ora might dance if you give her a big hand." They'd yell and whistle. Most of the time, they'd stand up and yell.

Then, Ora got up and danced. Everybody loved to see that. She could put on quite a show. It got around that she was as good a dancer as she was a musician. I'm sure that's why they wanted her over at the dance festival. I went and sat on stage and played the guitar. She got out there playing her fiddle and dancing at the same time. The audience loved it. I remember seeing her dancing around and her long, dark hair bouncing down her back.

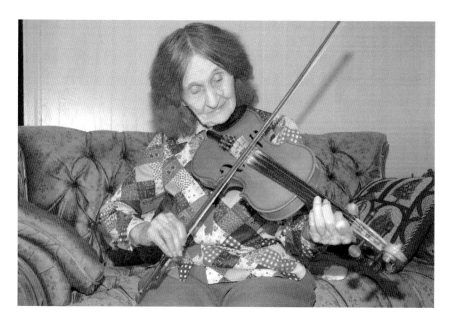

Ora is shown above in her living room giving an impromptu concert in November 2006. *Photograph by B. Salsi.*

Over the years, Ora developed an inner-ear problem. She'd want to dance but was afraid to play the fiddle too. Many times she'd dance and I'd hold on to her arm so she could balance and put in her original steps. Sometimes she'd do the Charleston.

Editor's note:
Ora Watson is one of the best-known musicians in Western North Carolina and Eastern Tennessee. She knows more old tunes and ballads than anyone I've ever met. I know her from attending many jam sessions at the senior citizens' center in Boone and in Cove Creek, North Carolina, with Glenn Bolick and Amy Michels. When she picks up her fiddle, there is nothing tentative about her performance. She plays effortlessly, as though tunes flow through her fingers. Most of all, she plays for the love of playing.

EULA RUSS OSBORNE

FARMER, LACEMAKER AND
GRANDMA'S DARLIN'

I was born in the Three Top community in Ashe County, North Carolina. We could see Three Top Mountain. That's somewhere near the other places that I lived—Roundabout, Cabbage Creek, Ashland and Trout. They are all small communities right near the Tennessee and North Carolina border. We always lived way back in the mountains. There was an altitude up in the three thousands, but there is no prettier bottomland to be found anywhere. It's good for growin' all kinds of crops, and that's what we did all my life.

There were few conveniences in the twenties, thirties and forties. That meant we did everything the hard way—by hand. The families that lived all 'round us were all the same—poor—but they managed to farm and get all the things they needed to support their families.

THE LITTLE STORE

My grandparents were Cora Goss and Granville Humphrey. Everybody knew 'em. Their house was set close to Roundabout Road right off the little dirt lane. The six-room house was built of weatherboarding. It was a right big house with the least little basement dug out under the high end. Grandma and Granddaddy run a little store out of the basement, despite it havin' a dirt floor. They sold flour and sugar and small things to people in the area. Back in those days, if you had a stock of 'baccer, snuff, crackers and such, that's all you needed. Those were just little things that'd help people out 'til they got to the general store.

Roundabout Road is still a windy, narrow road that connects to Highway 88 between Trade, Tennessee, and West Jefferson, North Carolina. Once paved, it was easier for residents near Three Top Mountain to have jobs outside of the community. *Photograph by B. Salsi.*

My grandmother inherited right smart of land. When she married Grandpa, they made their home where she'd lived all her life. She was an only child of Estelle Goss. Her daddy's land went all the way up Three Top Mountain. Once I walked over the top with her. It was something steep going up. We had to pull ourselves along by little saplings. Grandma had heard someone was plantin' on her land. She got up there and saw acres of 'taters. It didn't do much for her to tell the man, "That's my land." She wrote him a letter and then had to get a lawyer. The whole thing got settled when the man paid Grandma for the acres.

Granddaddy Humphrey was right lazy. That's not to say he didn't work at all. He'd get out workin' the farm. But he liked to take a lot of breaks, and when he got a chance, he'd have a drink with his friends. One day Granddaddy Granville had some friends stop by. After a little while, Grandma found out they was drinking down in the store. She didn't like that, so she got a gun and shot right down through the floor to break it up. They all scattered. From then on, they didn't drink anywhere Grandma would know about.

My aunt knew Granddaddy talked to himself a lot. She wanted to figure out what he was sayin'. One day she slipped behind the door when he was comin' in. He said, "Eh, lawdy, that bean patch is a crowdin' me to death." She got tickled and gave herself away. Granddaddy never understood what she was doin' there. From then on, he'd look behind the door when he came into the room.

GRANDMA DID EVERYTHING

My grandparents were farmers and Grandma kept the post office. She did that for twenty-seven years until she was too old to walk back and forth. She was the one who knew how to do everything. She held the family together and did most of the work. The little community of a few farms up and down the road was known as Solitude in the early days. My grandma said people had poured out so many piles of ashes on the road and near their houses she changed the name of the post office to Ashland because of the ash all around.

Grandma was doin' big farmin' and still going to the post office everyday. She and my granddaddy lived on the land Amy and Alfred Michels live on today. She got out and walked a mile to work. It wasn't too bad, but the post office department required the postmaster to open up despite the weather. Grandma would walk through three feet of snow, build a fire in the little wood stove and stay there all day, maybe sellin' only one three-cent stamp. On those ten-degree days, few people come by to check their mail.

The post office was set on a big rock below a little store up on Roundabout Road near Cabbage Creek. We had to walk over the rock to get into the store. The post office was a separate buildin' only about ten by twelve feet. It was an outbuildin' kind of shed. The space where Grandma took care of the mail was only about four feet by eight feet. She had little shelves for sortin'. When people came in for their mail, she had a little slot she could pass it through.

The young'uns weren't allowed in her walled-off space. She held to it that was "official United States post office" space—no one allowed unless they were post office or government people. There was a little wood-burning stove with a bench behind it. People gathered to warm themselves and wait for the mail to come in. Most days they'd sit around and pass the time tellin' stories and talkin' about their families while waitin'.

Even today, our little community is out of the way off of main roads. In the early 1900s, when there were no paved roads, the community was really hard to reach. The road ran from Trade, Tennessee, to West Jefferson, North Carolina. It was so windy and narrow it was hard to travel into the various communities along the way. After a rain it was worse, because it was muddy and unfit for travelin'. I think back to when I was a young'un. I remember the farmers travelin' up and down the road strugglin' through the mess tryin' to haul crops in horse-drawn wagons.

In Grandma's day, there wasn't much offered in the way of schoolin'. There might be a few months a year. She learned to read and write and 'cipher. If she were livin' today, people would say she was a genius. Several young'uns would come to the post office after school and she'd tutor their math.

DADDY COMES TO NORTH CAROLINA

My daddy, Dan Russ, came cross the mountain from Abingdon, Virginia, and met my mother, Maybell—Grandma Humphrey's daughter. They married and Mama moved to Virginia with Daddy. But, that only lasted for a little while before they were back in North Carolina. I was born when my brother, James, was almost four.

My mother died when I was ten months old. I was lucky she had asked my Aunt Elsie, her sister, to take care of my brother and me. Aunt Elsie

In Cora Goss Humphrey's day, most of the farmers used steer for the heavy hauling jobs.
When Eula was just a girl, she drove a yoke of steer to haul fodder. *Photograph courtesy of
the North Carolina Department of Archives and History.*

was a good mother to us. She ended up marrying my father. That's how she became my aunt and my stepmother. She said she figured marryin' Daddy was the best way she could take care of us. When Elsie and Daddy had six more children, they were my brothers and sisters and also my cousins. I loved my stepmother. She was the only mother I ever knew and I called her Mama. She was good to all of the young'uns—much better to us than our daddy.

WEST VIRGINIA

After they married, Dad talked Aunt Elsie into movin' to West Virginia. He went into minin'. It was talked around that men could get work that paid big money by workin' in the mines. The house he had there was little more than a shanty with three rooms, and we were never warm. While Daddy was there, some of men from the Ashland area went up. Daddy and Mama took 'em in. There wasn't enough room for everybody and one of 'em had to sleep on a cot in the kitchen.

I was only about three years old and was told about this by my mother. I was only there for six months, before I was sent to live with my grandmother. She didn't want me goin' in the first place. She was happy to have me live with her. When the coal fields went to the bad, Dad bought a car from his bosses and headed back to North Carolina.

Grandmama Humphrey had pretty much raised me from a baby. She meant everything to me, and I'd never been away from her before that time. I ended up stayin' with her most of the time until I was over ten years old. All her lessons were important to me all of my life. They helped me during hard times and were good things to pass on to my children.

Grandma only got to finish the fourth grade in school. Her mama died and she was needed to do things at home. That didn't mean she didn't get all the school she could. That's why she saw to it that I went to school. Our school year was six months and I made it through to the tenth grade. At the time, there were only eleven grades. I later went back and finished up.

When Daddy came back to North Carolina, he bought twenty acres and a house near Cabbage Creek for six hundred dollars in 1935. That was only about two miles from Grandma. As I got older, he was on me to come home and help out in the farmin' on his land. That put me farmin' with Grandma and with Daddy. I used to get out at 5:30 and work 'til dark. After that, I still had to milk the cow, feed the animals, cut wood and carry it in.

Hard Work

Daddy thought his young'uns needed to do all the work. Since James and I were much older than the children he raised with Elsie, a lot fell to us for a long time. He didn't worry about much of nothin', but he knew how to put us out doin' everything. Once I was sent up in the field with a yoke of oxen. Bill and Charlie were pullin' the sled and I was to fetch fodder to feed the cows. My mother went up with me, 'cause I was only about twelve years old. Bill got contrary and was bad to turn the yoke. He started actin' like he was chokin'.

It was hard for a small girl to get behind two big brutish animals. It made me mad to think I'd not get the job done and over with. I went to unfasten the yoke with my mother saying, "Let 'em go, let 'em go." I got Bill by the horns and fixed that yoke. I hollered at him and made him keep on goin' with the load.

I got no pay for all that. In the summer, I'd try to get time to run out and pull some herbs. I'd store 'em in the barn loft 'til I got enough to sell to get me a little money to buy myself a piece of cloth. My mother was good to help me sew a new dress. Goodness, people today don't know anything about what it was like to work like we had to.

We'd all get out in the field and start workin' together—Daddy and all the young'uns old enough to do something. When he saw somebody walkin' down the road, he'd leave us workin' and go over and talk as long as he wanted to. He didn't care that his children were workin' and he was loafin'. When I got up older, I got the nerve to tell my sister and brother, "Okay, when he stops, we'll just take a little break too." We sat down while he visited. He came over to us and said, "Why aren't you workin?" My brother James said, "Oh we thought we'd take a little break and rest."

We were brave to do that, because we were always worried about gettin' the "hickory tea." That meant Daddy would get a hickory stick and lay it on us. He'd say, "I'm gonna give ya some hickory tea." He might pull a switch two-and-a-half-feet long and a half-inch around. It had the little sprouts and all stickin' out. That was bad enough, but if Daddy got really mad, I got the belt. My mama 'ud run in between us to save me.

When we were young, Daddy wouldn't let us go to Sunday school. When he was in West Virginia, my grandmama took me to her church anyway. When we got older, Daddy got to be a better man. It helped that the preacher called on him a few times and caused him to see the light.

We went to both the Methodist and the Baptist church. Once the church was lookin' for a place to build. Dad said he'd give 'em the land if they agreed to give it back if the church closed or moved somewhere else. They didn't accept his offer.

Grandmother had the young'uns out teachin' us how to get rid of bean bugs and potato bugs. She would get an old tin. It was mostly a Prince Albert tobacco can with a lid that flipped back, yet was still hinged to the can. She'd put kerosene in it. We'd flip open the lid and drop in the bugs. She would give us a penny for five bugs. If we smashed a leaf full of eggs, we'd get a nickel. That was big money back then.

Grandmother taught us to milk cows and how to keep the milk cool. She sold milk every day when the calves didn't need it all. We had three large five-gallon cans with handles on either side. They were really heavy when full of milk. The milkman had a route to travel. He loaded the cans on a flatbed truck and took them to the milk plant. Some milk was used for cheese at the cheese plant in West Jefferson. Some was hauled to other places where it was canned.

At harvest time we used to can a thousand cans of beans, corn, carrots, soup, chicken, pork, sausage and beef. We picked apples and fixed 'em for applesauce and apple butter. It was all kept in the basement on shelves built in the corner. We also dried apples and used 'em later in pies.

Fresh applesauce was so good. I'd peel the apples and cook 'em on the stove. When they were soft, I'd strain 'em. After I added sugar and spices, the applesauce was put in jars and sealed. I loved to take a biscuit and spread it with applesauce. Then I'd add three or four layers. It was like a small cake and so good. It was only better if we could skim some cream off the top of milk and make some whipped cream to put on top.

We liked eatin' the cottage cheese we made. After skimmin' off the cream, I'd set out the milk and let it clabber. Then, I'd let it simmer and drain the water off. Next I'd add a little salt and butter and let it cool. It'd be delicious cottage cheese. Store-bought milk won't make it. It takes fresh milk without any chemicals added.

Christmas

My grandma got me everything at Christmas. My Daddy got me nothin. She got me a store-bought doll with a ribbon tied in its hair. I usually got some clothes. They were secondhand, not new, but they were nice. She picked 'em out from the things shipped by barrels into Ennos Osborne's store on Roundabout Road.

She bought things for all the grand-young'uns. There were also homemade toys, like a monkey on a string, doll beds, sleds, doll clothes, wooden cars and paper dolls.

I didn't get a Christmas tree at my parents' house until I was twelve. I went out in the woods and cut it and put it up by myself. I sprangled it out with some balloons I had. Then, I popped some popcorn for my younger brothers and sisters and we made long strings. Daddy ignored it all, but Mother was real pleased and the young'uns were so excited about Christmas.

PARTY TIME

Five or six times a year, Grandma invited a whole bunch of young people over to her house. They came from all over. Most of the young'uns weren't used to havin' sweets, so they looked forward to comin' over. Grandma would play the fiddle and get a Charleston dance goin'. Everybody wanted to come. She'd make a batch of taffy and boil it 'til it got a little stiff. Then she'd get us to pullin' it 'til it turned white. One of the ladies that came one day got to pullin' 'til the candy snapped and got in her eyebrow. We almost never got it out. We washed and washed.

We looked forward to corn shuckin' held in the fall. If a boy found the speckled ear, he could kiss the girl of his choice. If a girl found it, she could give a kiss. It was all in fun and most times the person findin' the ear was too embarrassed to do kissin' in front of everybody. There was a lot of laughin' and teasin'.

CONVENIENCES

All this was before we had electricity and a telephone. They were not available, even if we wanted them. We washed our clothes on a scrub board—a zigzag board. We rubbed our clothes up and down until they were clean. Sometimes this wore blisters on our hands and it wore the fabric out pretty quick. We had to hang our clothes outside and depend on the sunshine to get our things dry.

Then, we ironed our clothes with old cast-iron irons that were heated on the stove where we did our cooking. We had four irons. They weighed about two or three pounds. It was hard work, but once they were heated, we could do a good job ironing. When one iron got cold and couldn't get the wrinkles out, we put it back on the stove to reheat and picked up a hot iron. We switched until the job was done. It sometime took the whole day for the ironing.

If we had more than we could finish in one day, the clothes were sprinkled with water we poured in an empty soda pop bottle with holes punched in the lid. We tied them up in a sheet to iron later. Havin' all those cotton clothes damp helped them to iron nicely.

We didn't have runnin' water in the house. There was a tank on the side of the wood cook stove that held about ten gallons of water. We carried buckets of water from the spring to fill the tank twice a day. We had to heat water on the stove to have hot water for washing dishes and takin' baths.

Only rich people had a bathroom. We had an outside toilet and a number-three tub made of zinc to bath in. It was fine for children, but it was hard for adults to get their legs into the tub. Parents took their children out before bed to use the bathroom. This meant several trips if there were a lot of kids. Our two-holer had a large hole for adults to sit on and a smaller hole next to it for the children to use. This went on my entire childhood and even after I married.

After I got married, my husband, Vernon, came in and said, "This is it. I've had enough. I'm going to get a second job, so we can build a bathroom."

The electricity only went as far as Riverview. We had to wait until it reached us. There was no telephone, either. When we needed to make a call, we had to go all the way to Warrensville, about seven miles down the road toward West Jefferson.

WOMEN'S WORK

We had sewin' machines with pedals to make them go. This was better than my grandmother and great-grandmother had it. They had only a needle and thread. But we got cloth—some from one of the little old stores and some from savin' feed sacks. Neither offered much choice in pattern and color. We did the best way we could and made everything that everybody wore. Pedalin' that machine all day made our legs and ankles tired. Now, people collect 'em as a curiosity, but I remember being happy to get one that ran on electricity. If you're doin' sewing all day, it saves a lot of effort.

Back then, women had it all on them. They had to birth the young'uns, raise 'em, cook for everybody, do cannin', totin', feedin' animals, milkin' cows, pickin' beans and corn and diggin' 'taters. There was a feelin' what was women's work and what was men's work. There was plenty of hard work in plowin', clearin' land, plantin' crops and butcherin' that men did, but my granddaddy and daddy left too much to the women and children. They weren't of a mind to help if you were doin' work that they considered women's work. They were also glad to get a few young'uns up old enough to cut wood and haul it to stack on the porch or close to the house. The young'uns knew not to be reminded to do their chores. They got up and did 'em just the same as takin' time to eat or puttin' on clothes. To be reminded might mean a whoopin'—and you'd still have the work.

Ladies took care of all the beddin'. We made cotton tick covers to stuff to make mattresses. We raised ducks and stuffed the ticks with feathers to help keep us warm on cold nights. Then we made quilts by hand from scraps we'd saved. Sometimes we had a lot of fun gettin' neighbor people together to work on different people's quilts on different days.

I helped make quilts—some with my fingers and some on the sewing machine. Nearly sixty years ago I'd quilt a quilt for $1.50. That was after they made the top and tacked the three layers together. It wasn't much for so many hours of work, but that was the time you'd be lucky to make 50¢ a day workin' for others in the field. We got 25¢ a bushel for pickin' beans. We were glad when it went up to 50¢.

When it was zero weather outside, we'd cover ourselves from head to toe before we went out. One time my mother didn't want me to go out and haul in wood by myself 'cause there was so much ice on the ground. She was afraid I might fall and not be able to make it back and I might freeze to death. She went with me, but before we left the house she lined our boots with paper. She said it'd help keep out the cold.

Grandma was good to get the old irons heated on the stove. She wrapped them up in towels and put them to our feet to help us get warm in the cold bed. I've never forgotten the lovin' extra things she did.

We didn't keep too much fire going at night. We were afraid the soot in the flue would spark up and catch on fire. Grandma's old, wood weather-sidin' house would have burned down in a hurry. This was part of the things that were handed down to us that taught us how to survive. Many of the mountain people my age and younger still burn wood to keep their homes warm. They were brought up knowing how to cut wood and haul it—and everybody knows how to build a fire.

My brother and I were the ones to keep wood ahead. Mama couldn't do much as she started havin' children. When she married Daddy, she took James and me as her own. Eventually, she and Daddy had six more. All the young'uns learned to saw up trees and stack and haul in wood.

Everybody cut trees down to clear the land to plant food for the family, cattle, chickens and hogs. The brush was taken to a place where they were going to sow seedbeds, like tobacco beds and beds for plants for the garden. It was burned to help kill weeds so the seeds could grow. We planted corn in the new ground. We couldn't plow that new clear land, so we used a hoe and made a hole about every three feet and planted three grains of corn in it. If all three came up, the middle one was pulled up to leave room for the others to have plenty of food and sunshine. This is why the old folks called corn bread "two in a hill."

There weren't much fertilizer. Even if we could find it at a store, we couldn't afford it. Ashes from burnin' wood in fireplaces and woodstoves were strewn over the land. We also used cow manure, horse manure and chicken manure.

Sometimes, boxes—made large enough to hold about a bushel of manure—were set up on four stobs and a hole was cut in the corner of the box. A corncob was plugged in the hole. Then, the box was filled with water to let it soak for about four hours. When it was ready, the box was tilted so one corner was a little lower and the hole was unplugged. The liquids drained down to the corner opening and caught in buckets. The drainin's were poured around the plants to help them grow better.

There were few cars on the road. The roads were more like cow paths. Grass grew up in the middle and on the sides of the roads. There was only one main road, which is now called Highway 88. In those days, it was called the "sand road," 'cause in dry weather it was nothing but sand. When it rained, cars and trucks got stuck in the mud. They had to be pulled out by oxen or horses, because there were almost no tractors in our community.

The school bus could hardly make it through to pick up students, and traveled slow through the mud and ruts. If a young'un was runnin' late gettin' out to meet the bus, he could run down the road and catch up to the bus. Those on the back seat acted as lookouts. When they saw someone runnin' after it, they'd holler for the bus driver to stop.

One time, one of the school buses got stuck. Mr. Wade Eller made pictures of the bus being pulled out by oxen and sent them to Raleigh. He had the senior class write letters to Raleigh about the road conditions. That got things rollin' and caused the sand road to become Highway 88.

Vernon

I met Vernon when he went to Grandma's church. I was headin' home, walkin' down the road with my aunts. He was pickin' at another girl and gave her some flowers. Then he walked up to me and said he wanted to walk me home to Grandma's. I was sixteen. We got there and he said, "When can I see you next?"

There was nowhere to go in our county; everybody courted by goin' out walkin'. Daddy acted ugly. He didn't like it that I was out walkin' with a boy. Once Vernon came over to see me and we were sittin' in the parlor. After a while, Mother motioned to me. She said, "Tell him to leave. Your dad's actin' ugly."

I went back in and said to Vernon, "I'll see you later." He caught on and got up and left.

It wasn't long after that when we were walkin home from church and he asked me to marry him. A few weeks later he said his cousin would take us to Mountain City, Tennessee, where they didn't require us to have a blood test. We were figurin to sneak over on Monday. There was no way I wanted Daddy to know about it. I put my good dress in the bottom of the water bucket and then set another bucket on it. I had everything ready. I could say I was goin' out to hunt berries and take off from there.

My aunt had a car. On Sunday, the day before I was runnin' off with Vernon, I decided to ride from Grandma's to Daddy's with my two aunts, my daddy and my aunt's boyfriends from Bristol, Tennessee. We went down the road and they got a flat tire near Dr. Robinson's office. Daddy got out and said that he'd just walk on home about a quarter-mile away. Then, he said, "Eula, come with me."

My aunt spoke up and said, "Why can't she ride with us?"

Daddy walked on off and I was standin' around watchin' the tire get changed. In a few minutes, Vernon happened by. He said, "Are you ready to go? My brother-in-law can take us on over to Tennessee."

"I was thinkin you said we'd go tomorrow." I was scared. But I went on with him. I was lookin' back every curve to see if Dad was followin' us. We got married at the home of the justice of the peace.

Somebody told Dad we were gettin' married. He tried to get someone to take him to go after us, but nobody would help him. Then he walked over to Grandma's and acted like he didn't know where I was. Grandma said, "She's gone to get married." She handed him a cabbage and said, "Go on home and fix a wedding supper."

He didn't do anything. My mother-in-law fixed a nice supper and we lived with her and my father-in-law for about two years. It wasn't too bad, except my mother-in-law would snap me off sometime. Her husband didn't argue with her. He just said, "yah, yah, yah." Then he went on about his business.

The Flood

In April of 1940, the year of the big flood, it rained and rained and didn't seem like it would ever stop. The ground couldn't hold any more water and we knew there were some bust-outs and landslides comin' off some of the mountains. The worst was when the Tater Hill dam broke and rushed down Howard's Creek. That and the rain caused floods everywhere.

People were helpless. There was no electricity in the mountains and no way for people to get the word to get to higher ground. With no radio and no warnin' system, it was a matter of hearin' the noise, seein' the water rise or havin' a neighbor come to see about ya and help ya get away. It washed away houses and people died.

Ethel Lewis went over to her daddy-in-law's to get to higher ground. Her husband put their hog in the house to keep it from being washed away. They were lookin' out the window at the rain and Warren said, "There goes our house and our hog too." The house washed down the valley and they lost everything.

There was great sufferin'. But neighbor helped neighbor and eventually people built back and planted fields. It took years for things to get normal. Some never got over it and left the mountains.

A Place of Our Own

We found us a small farm and house near Three Top Mountain. We had nine children and seven lived. We always farmed heavy—fifteen acres of beans, five acres of corn, four acres of 'baccer. In those days, we'd sell our 'baccer over in West Jefferson, North Carolina or Mountain City, Tennessee. Not many people grow it anymore; they can't sell it like that anymore.

Vernon could do anything—cook, farm, sew. He made the best husband and father. He also played music. He'd get his guitar and I'd get my mandolin. Some evenin's we'd sit on the porch swing and play and sing.

From the day we married, Vernon tried gettin' me out of the field. But I wanted to show Dad I could do more in the field than he could. We kept on farmin' even though Vernon and I took outside jobs. Sometime we hired ourselves out to work in the neighbor's fields spuddin' and cuttin' 'baccer. I was twenty-one and Dad was workin' with us. He told someone that his young'un nearly "covered him up" in work. That was the only time he ever gave me a compliment. But he was out workin' hard those days, 'cause he

Eula and Vernon built
a little old house to
move in after they
lived with relatives
for a few years. Over
the years the house
expanded with the
birth of children.
*Photograph courtesy of the
Osborne collection.*

Eula and Vernon
enjoyed playing
instruments and
creating a little
entertainment for
themselves and for
their family. This is
Eula's photo. She
said, "This is a picture
of Vernon acting
the fool." *Photograph
courtesy of the Osborne
collection.*

Vernon and Eula farmed heavy from the beginning of their marriage. This is a photo of the couple when Eula was age twenty-one. *Photograph courtesy of the Osborne collection.*

Eula and Vernon were married for ten years before they took a two-day vacation to Wilkesboro. Eula is pictured above in front of the cabin they stayed in. *Photograph courtesy of the Osborne collection.*

was workin' for money. We cut several crops that year. Vernon helped by drivin' sticks for dryin' the 'baccer.

We were always workin' to get ahead. When we were young, we milked six cows a day and sold the milk to help pay for our land. We also got a bonus out of not havin' to buy milk or butter for our young'uns. We milked the cows and then set a fine wire strainer on top of the milk can and poured the milk in, strainin' any dirt or trash out of the milk. We filled the milk can half full and set it in the deepest part of the water in our coolin' trough we built in the creek.

We had the first part only two inches deep for butter and twelve inches deep for the milk cans. When only half-filled, the milk stayed real cool. We filled the cans right before the truck came by. We hauled the cans to the truck on a special wheelbarrow that Vernon fixed. Each can had our initials on it, so the milkman knew where to leave the empties the next mornin'. We were paid by the cheese factory in West Jefferson. They sent us a check every two weeks. Milk was picked up six days a week, just not on Sunday. We kept the milk from Sunday cool and had it ready for pick up on Monday.

We were married ten years before we got to take off anywhere. We went to North Wilkesboro for a little two-day vacation and stayed in a cottage. That's where they had the movies ya could see in the car. I'd heard of 'em. It was really something to sit in our car and see my first movie.

Followin' Tradition

Doctors came in more after I was married, but I learned a lot about cures from Grandma. She'd boil the needles from a spruce pine tree she had next to the road. Then she strained the liquid and put sugar in it. Next, she boiled it down and made cough medicine. She'd give it to us by the spoonful for our coughs and colds.

Catnip tea was made to help give us a good night's sleep and rest. It was so good to give the fussy babies. I gave it to all my young'uns. Boneset tea was good for colds. We grew a big patch and sold some. We also drank Penny Royal tea.

I bought most of my clothes from money I saved from sellin' herbs and such. My brother James and I would go out and get May apple, elderflower and boneset. We'd dry it and shave the little flowers from the elderflower. We might skin some cherry bark. We'd take it to Ennos Osborne's store. He bought the herbs. Sometimes we just traded for a

Eula is an expert lace maker in the old mountain tradition. The art has been passed from one generation to another. *Photograph by B. Salsi.*

Eula uses two skeins of pure cotton thread to "knit" her beautiful bed canopies. The special needles are now plastic, but used to be hand carved. *Photographs by B. Salsi.*

Beautiful bed canopies are the finished product of hours and hours of "knitting" lace by hand. *Photograph by B. Salsi.*

piece of cloth or something we needed. Once Grandma was with me and she bought me the prettiest dress I ever saw. It was blue with an embroidered band at the waist. It had a sash tied in the back. It was just like new. I think she paid a quarter for it.

Knittin' and Tasselin'

Since I retired twenty-five years ago, I've been makin' lace for bed canopies sold all over the world. Makin' lace is an old mountain traditional craft. People have passed the knowledge down from generation to generation. My daughter-in-law and sister showed me how to do it. First, I get a stick the right size to wrap thread around. The first time it took me two weeks to do one strip. Now I can make three or four a week.

I started out workin' for a lady in Todd but now my son sells 'em. I call it "knottin' and tasselin'." At one time a lot of people around here did it for extra money. It was a small opportunity for mountain women to make a little cash. Sometimes I get going and knit the lace for eighteen hours at a time. The pay isn't much, but, at my age, the little I get comes in good.

Once the right number of knots is made usin' a shuttle and a handmade wooden frame, it becomes a long piece of lace. When I started, the shuttles, or what some call "needles," were made by whittlin' it from wood. Now, I can buy 'em made from plastic. They don't wear out.

When the piece is the way I want it, I hand wash it and hang it up to dry. It is made of two strands of fine cotton, so the washin' causes 'em to shrink. That tightens the mesh and gets the pieces the right size for the bed size. It takes 13,000 knots for a king-size and 9,050 knots for a queen. After the pieces for the sides and top are put together, the canopy is finished off with hundreds of tassels. I don't do the tasselin'—my daughter and some other people do that.

Some people have told me it's a lot like knittin' a fishin' net. To me, it's knots and fringe. There are no written directions. It all comes with practice of how to get the hand tying smooth and even. I'm of a mind to get up every day and start on the lace right after breakfast.

Editor's Note:
Eula Osborne is a remarkable lady. She worked all her life doing farmwork and raising children. She still managed to complete her high school education and attended a year of college. She worked an outside job for over twenty-five years and juggled that with milking cows, feeding animals, raising children and helping with grandchildren. Up until the summer of 2006, she canned thousands of jars of food for her family. However, her pressure cooker exploded, destroyed her kitchen and nearly killed her. She spent weeks in the hospital. She returned to her lace knitting and makes beautiful bed canopies. For the first time in her life, she's not thinking about canning.

In the early 1900s, some families farmed and raised their families in one- or two-room houses. *Photographs courtesy of the North Carolina Department of Archives and History.*

CLYDE LEWIS

TURKEY FARMER, BLUES MUSICIAN AND MILKMAN

I was born way up in the holler. I grew up as the third of seven brothers, when times weren't much more than workin' to stay alive, and people were out workin' for next to nothin'. We all pitched in helpin' with farmin', and raisin' cows and chickens. It took a lot to feed nine people.

CASH CROP

We grew a lot of things to eat—most all our eatin'. Mama and Daddy had cows and chickens. We butchered and put the meat up in barrels. We planted, hoed, picked and dug. Mama worked hard to keep the can house full. We didn't grow much extra, maybe a little we could trade some of what we had for something we needed. It was hard to grow enough to feed nine people.

We never had a lot to eat. I don't remember us ever havin' enough to eat to make us feel full. It wouldn't have been hard to go out and eat everything in the can house. But we were afraid of starvation, and Mama knew just how to be careful to make it last us through the winter. Daddy and the older boys would hunt and then we might have coon, squirrel or groundhog to eat.

Our cash crop was turkeys, but we never ate one. We herded turkeys like herding sheep. All the families in our community did the same. Each family notched their turkeys' feet to keep up with 'em. Ours were notched on the middle toe on the left foot. We were all tryin' to raise all we could.

Fast streams were important to early farmers. This one creates a picturesque setting for the little house (left) in front of Clyde and Ruth's where Clyde sometimes sits and reminisces. *Photograph by B. Salsi.*

Clyde's daddy sharecropped on seven different farms and raised flocks of turkeys. The Lewis boys worked with their daddy to support the family. *Photograph courtesy of the Lewis collection.*

We let 'em out to eat what they could find. It got rough if your turkey got out on someone else's place. They were roamin' fowl, but it was important to keep 'em off the land of others. They might kill your turkey. Sometimes people wouldn't take too much notice of a property line if there were a lot of grasshoppers. Turkeys would swarm all over eatin' up the grasshoppers.

Once, my brothers and I drove our turkeys up where we saw a lot of grasshoppers. We knew it was okay to take 'em there. We took a nigh cut through neighbor's property that wouldn't mind. We thought we'd leave 'em there to eat. But when we headed down off the ridge, we saw the turkeys followin' behind us. Turkeys know where their home is. They might wander around a little, but they'd come on back home.

We had to drive the turkeys to Highway 88 down Roundabout Road to where people would come to buy whole flocks. As we herded our turkeys down the road, others along the way joined in. We'd go on down toward the meetin' point where the turkeys would be weighed. It'd be like drivin' 'em, except they were turkeys, not cattle. What a sound those thousands of turkeys made. We could hear 'em cacklin' for a mile.

We made about 3¢ a pound. It was the money from the sale of the turkeys that got us our clothes and shoes and sugar and coffee and stuff needed we couldn't grow.

It was the worst if the turkeys got cholera. It was called the "black head." Their heads turned black. The turkeys would wander off and die. The sick ones followed the well. That would take out the whole flock and then there'd be nothing for our family to live on except the food in the cellar house. We'd barely get by.

The good years we'd keep our seed—five hens and a tom turkey. That'd be the next year's crop. They'd make their nests beginning in March and on. They don't lay in the winter. Once we had a turkey hen we kept in the chicken house because we wanted to save her. She laid eggs and they hatched out and there hadn't been a tom around for a long time.

One turkey could lay a hundred eggs—one a day. We counted on our seed turkeys to give us a big flock to sell.

Livin' Off the Land

People didn't have mattresses. They thrushed big piles of fresh straw and then they'd get enough to fill a tick to use as a mattress. I remember seein'

Large gardens provide food for the can house. J.T. Riggs is shown in Clyde and Ruth's garden in 2002. *Photograph courtesy of the Lewis collection.*

people walkin' up and down the road with a tick goin' to get fresh straw. Then they'd be walkin' back home with the full mattress on their backs.

Daddy knew how to do everything. He could make our brooms and chairs. He'd go out and get hickory. Then he'd peel or shave the bark back in different ways. They were called scrub brooms. They were handy for scrubbing wooden floors. It's a pity he couldn't sell 'em. But most everybody else knew how to make their own.

People also grew broomcorn. It grows like cane. The broom part is the head with seed on it. It comes out like a corn tassel with seeds all at the end. The seed is cut out. Several heads are used. They're put on a sturdy stick or pole by tying one this way and one that way.

Havin' a molasses boilin' was sometimes a chance to get together with neighbors for a social. The feller that owned the can mill and ground up the cane for molasses would charge a toll as his fee for his work and equipment. There was a lady in our neighborhood who owed him three gallons of molasses for her fee or toll. She insisted on countin' out the amount in cups. She's the only person I know who got three gallons into two one-gallon jugs. They went back and forth with each other, with the woman insistin' she knew how many cups there were in a gallon.

My brother and I heard about how the lady got the best of the molasses man when Daddy sharecropped near the Sutherland place. Once we busted wood all day long for that woman, thinkin' we'd get a little pay.

When we finished, she brought out two empty Prince Albert cans with the bottoms cut off to fix a can for matches. We didn't have matches and wouldn't have been allowed to carry 'em if we had 'em. We took the cans and went on and after that we were a little more careful about knowin' something about what we'd get paid.

Aside of growin' our eatin', we sometimes had to get out and find our own cures for sickness. There weren't any doctors. We had to figure things out for ourselves. A lot of the things that grew wild helped to relieve our ailments. Some people around made moonshine mixed with honey or herbs and helped with coughs. We were given boneset tea that was made from dried boneset leaves and water. It tasted so bitter, we begged for Mama to spare sugar or honey to help us get it down. It was good for colds and fever.

We were also given spicewood tea, Penny Royal tea and catnip tea. When we had a chest cold, Mama might give us a chest rub with groundhog oil or polecat grease. Usin' rendered skunk fat for anything was awful and I'm glad to say we didn't get that treatment often.

For poison oak blisters, we'd rub some creek mud on it. I worked with a feller who would eat it. He brought some poison oak to work with him. He said, "Here, eat it." A girl had some poison oak on her hand and he talked her into eatin' a little. She later said it helped stop the poison oak.

MAKIN' MONEY

People would do all kinds of things to make a little money. I worked cuttin' timber for seventy-five cents a day. But, back then ya could buy a lot of flour for that. They'd get out killin' rabbits and sellin' the fur at one of the stores. They'd go in and collect their 10¢ for each one. The man at the store would pitch 'em over in the corner 'til a feller came and hauled 'em off. If you'd go in to buy something, that corner had a pretty raunchy smell.

It was a usual thing for people to eat coon, squirrels and groundhogs. Back then, there were so many coons, people killed 'em to eat. Then, some of the fur might sell as much as five dollars each. Polecat wasn't eaten, but their fur would sell.

That gets me to thinkin' how we always heard there's a place on top of Three Top Mountain where rattlesnakes are in there thick. I'm not thinkin' to say names, but I've heard of a few people that would go up on the mountain and get snakes. Some were sold to religious groups that taught about snake handlin'. Some people caught and sold black snakes to farmers for as much as ten dollars each for gettin' rid of rats and other pests around their place.

Young'uns

School lasted six months of the year. I finished year seven, which was all we had. School was different then. If parents needed their young'uns home to hoe corn, then the young'uns hoed corn. All the young'uns stayed out a lot. Most did what they had to do to help out at home and then went on back to school. There wasn't much about a law makin' young'uns go to school, but if the teacher thought ya was just lyin' out, somebody might come after ya.

Some of my brothers went to the old school up on Roundabout Road. Teachers were interested in teaching us. It was thought the teachers had a good paying job, and it was. It was regular pay, but some teachers boarded with families for the period of time they stayed in our community. We had to pass our work. The teacher kept us repeating it until we got it.

Bad language was not accepted. They didn't teach any vulgar stuff. Now they teach stuff in school that we'd get a whoopin' for. If we got in trouble at school, we'd get another paddlin' when we got home.

We liked to run around a lot if we had a break from school. Playin' fox and hound would run ya to death. If you were a fox you'd run and run tryin' to outfox the hounds. The boys that were hounds would run ya 'til they caught ya. Then he'd have to be the fox.

When I was a young'un, I might have ten cents sometimes and I'd go to Clyde Allen's store and get a big bag of candy. Now ten cents wouldn't pay the tax on a bag of candy. When they widened out the road to pave it, the store was in the way—right on the road curve—and it got torn down.

Once a year the circus would come through, down Roundabout Road as it moved from Mountain City, Tennessee, to Jefferson or somewhere in that area. I'm not sure where it ended up, because we didn't have the money for a ticket nor a way to get there. But it all moved on foot. It came down the road with the wagons pulled by horses.

The wild animals were in cages and it was something to see lions and tigers. The road was usually muddy and real swampy. It was hard for everything to get free. The elephants came last and they were the best of all. My brothers and I were lined up on the fence watchin' it all. A man ridin' an elephant come along and said, "Ya better get off the fence, or the elephant might snout ya off."

GOIN' TO CHURCH

We went to the Big Valley Baptist church. That was the place to go to see our neighbors and get a little religion. The preacher came just about every week. He preached in more than one church on Sundays. The preachers made a little money, but not much. They mostly got handouts from the members. The big thing was to have the preacher come to your house. They always liked to eat fried chicken. The preacher never came to see us; we were too poor.

One Sunday, my brother and I were walkin' the nigh way to church by cuttin' over the mountain. We heard something scream. I said nothin'. My brother said nothin'. We just kept walkin'.

Then the scream came again. It seemed to be right at us. I looked at my brother and saw the look on his face. He was as scared as me. Rather than run, I said, "Do you want to go on to church or do you want to go back home?" I could tell he was glad I asked. After that, we took another path to church.

We hated to lie out. There wasn't any other place to go but church. If you didn't show up, somebody would likely think you were lyin' out.

It wasn't unusual for people to walk eight miles to get to church, especially if they were partial to a certain religion. The Baptists might walk two or three miles past a Methodist church because they were Baptist. That was the same for all the faiths.

The Missionary Baptists had revivals in Big Valley. They'd have foot washes. When we knew we were going to a revival night, my brothers and I took care to wash our feet before we went. The feet-washin' members would come and set on the bench. They eased over your feet, but it was part of the belief.

HOME

All us boys lived at home 'til we got married, but we moved seven times before I left home. Daddy was mostly sharecroppin'. He didn't own any land. He'd move on somebody's property and farm the land for a share of the harvest. We'd live in the landowner's rentin' house. Daddy was good to work and all the boys got out workin' to help. He'd move on when he thought the move might be a better deal.

Three of my brothers and I played music and sang. We performed as the Wonder Valley Boys. We did pretty well as professional entertainers and got invited to play a lot of places on the weekends. We were in

Clyde married Ruth, a Tennessee girl, and brought her to Roundabout Road. Clyde and Ruth are shown above in 1984. *Photograph courtesy of the Lewis collection.*

Tennessee a lot and went as far as Mississippi. We got paid most of the time, but there were times we'd play for a meal and travel money. We started playin' bluegrass when it was modern music. It was a new sound compared to what everybody was used to.

Daddy bought a 78-record. He cranked up our talkin' machine and we loved hearin' that music. Before we got a radio, we walked from under the peak to Oscar Elliott's to hear Ralph Stanley, Delmore Brothers, Bill Monroe and the Carter Family. Then we sat for hours and listened to Fibber McGee and Molly. The biggest thing was hearin' the Grand Ole Opry broadcast live from Nashville.

I met my wife, Ruth, when I was playin' guitar in Bluff City, Tennessee, over near Bristol. There was a store where they'd clear out an area in the back and have us come over and play. Her sister had heard us play before and told Ruth to come over and hear us.

We went over there quite a few times, and each time I'd see Ruth. She had the same kind of life I had. She knew about raisin' animals and plantin' and plowin'. She was pretty young, but had a lot of responsibility. I was twenty-eight when we married in 1952.

We moved on Roundabout Road in a little bitty two-room house. I told Ruth there'd be preachin' at our house on Sunday. She said she didn't know how since the place was so small. But she did her best to make a little room and set out what few chairs we had.

A few neighbors came over and sat down. Then a man come in—the preacher. He went up to the front of the room and says, "It's 'gin the law to smoke. It's 'gin the law to drink. But, it's not 'gin the law to chew."

By then, everybody started laughing and Ruth knew I'd played a big joke on her.

We followed the life we'd known. I worked extra and had a milk route for a long time. I bought a truck 'specially to haul the milk to the plant in Jefferson. I drove from house to house and picked up each family's milk that was in ten-gallon milk cans. Each family had their number on their cans. After the milk was poured out at the plant, the cans were cleaned and delivered back to the customers the next day when I picked up their full cans.

After they milked the cows, the milk had to be strained to get dirt out of it. If it had trash in it, the plant wouldn't accept it. It was hard to tell customers they weren't gettin' paid for all their hard work. Some would swear I got their milk dirty. I hauled some for the preacher's wife. She got so mad when she didn't collect pay because of the dirt in her milk. She said, "I used a strainer."

But there was an outtin' cloth that was better than a metal mesh strainer. When put over the can openin' it'd strain out all dirt, no matter how small. I bought her a piece. She used it and saw that dirt had been gettin' in her milk. She come out and apologized and thanked me for buyin' her the cloth. Some people would use the fabric from a ham sack, but the outtin' was the best of all.

I enjoyed driving my milk route and made a lot of friends. During the time I had it, some families bought a cow when they found out they could make a little money. When I sold my route, I went to work at the Broyhill furniture plant in Lenoir.

Livin' With Animals

When I married Ruth, she shared my interest in animals. We've always had cows, chickens, pigs, horses and such. We once had a hog that got way too big and fat. He liked to go up the hill in the heat of the day to find shade. Finally, he got too big to do that. I was thinkin' he might have a heart attack. One day, he went up and didn't come down. I found him and soaked him down with a bucket of water to get him cooled off. He got the strength to come down.

Before we could butcher, the hog died and we buried him at the edge of the 'baccer patch where the plants grew real puny. For the longest time, grease came up out of the ground and ran quite a ways. When we planted 'baccer the next year, it grew the best 'baccer plants we'd ever had there.

Once Ruth had a pet coon she named Billy. That's when we were livin' over at Graybeal Holler. She had it in a long cage and kept fresh leaves in it for Billy's bed. It was something. It knew its name and it loved to eat cookies. When one of us opened his door I'd say, "just stay there, Billy, and let me feed ya." Sometimes when I fed him, he'd bite me, and then he'd eat. He never bit Ruth. I guessed she was his favorite. Sometime we'd give him a fresh hen egg. He loved it. Once we thought to tease him a little and gave him a Guinea egg. Its shell is a lot harder than a regular hen egg. He looked at it, and then put his foot on it to crack it. He never did get it cracked and we had to crack it for him.

I like animals, but I can't stand a snake around me. My daddy told me that snakes protect their babies by swallowin' 'em back up. He said he was down at gravels at the creek and he saw a big black snake that scared him, but he musta scared the snake worse. He said the big ol' snake opened its mouth and swallowed up its young'uns.

Usually farm people tolerate black snakes, which keep a lot of pests like rats and such away from the house and barns. But black snakes also like to eat eggs and will go after little ducks and chickens. Most of the farmers keep on the lookout to keep their fowl safe.

One day I found a snake in the chicken nest where the hen had been settin'. The eggs were about ready to hatch, but the snake had swallered all six. We killed the snake and cut it open and got the eggs out. We put 'em back in the nest under the hen. When the eggs hatched, the ones that were in the snake never ate or drank. They ran around and around in circles 'til they died.

GOING HUNTIN'

I used to like huntin'. I'd go fox huntin'. I liked to hear the dogs a-runnin' and a-yappin'. Fox huntin' is something to do for fun, 'cause the dogs never get the fox, but a coon will get up a tree. The only way ya can find it is with a flashlight at night. But even then, if it covers its eyes, ya can't see it at all. The coon's eyes shine when the light hits 'em, and that gives away its hidin' place.

The animals have to be fed, even on 15-degree days with snow on the ground and the wind blowing thirty-five to forty miles per hour. (left to right) Ruth Lewis, Amy Michels, Lynn Salsi. *Photograph by B. Salsi.*

THE GOOD LIFE

Sometimes I think it was a better life back then than it is now. Everybody knew everybody, and we visited back and forth. We worked hard, but we took time to sit on the front porch and talk and play a little music. Even the times we nearly worked ourselves to death, everybody was willin' to get out and help their neighbors.

Ruth and Clyde Lewis enjoy farm life. They love humor and share stories about the way things were in the old days. *Photograph by B. Salsi.*

Editor's Note:

Clyde and Ruth Lewis have had a long and happy marriage. It has been amply seasoned with humor and teamwork. They've lived the kind of farm life that is quickly disappearing. Clyde's life shows another side of mountain life, one in which their main crop was turkeys. This was a community tradition, one that is not found many other places outside Avery County. Also, Clyde's family was among the thousands of hardworking mountain people who sharecropped because they couldn't afford to own their own land, even though it was only a few dollars an acre.

In his day, Clyde was a brilliant, much sought-after musician. He was glad to make a few bucks for each gig. He lived in a time when it was more about the music than the money. But he says it was good to get a little money and a free meal. By today's standards, he'd be in demand on major stages. When he was young, most of the opportunities for musicians were personal appearances in small venues including barn dances, rooms in the back of stores and summertime concerts on front porches.

Visit us at
www.historypress.net